DATE DUE

Teen Smoking

OTHER BOOKS OF RELATED INTEREST

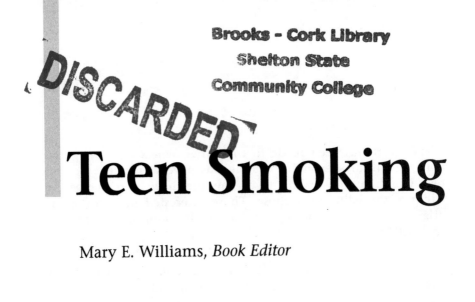

Teen Smoking

Mary E. Williams, *Book Editor*

David L. Bender, *Publisher*
Bruno Leone, *Executive Editor*
Bonnie Szumski, *Editorial Director*
David M. Haugen, *Managing Editor*
Brenda Stalcup, *Series Editor*

Contemporary Issues
Companion

Greenhaven Press, Inc., San Diego, CA

Library of Congress Cataloging-in-Publication Data

Teen smoking / Mary E. Williams, book editor.
    p.   cm. — (Contemporary issues companion)
  Includes bibliographical references and index.
  ISBN 0-7377-0169-2 (lib. : alk. paper). —
ISBN 0-7377-0168-4 (pbk. : alk. paper)
  1. Teenagers—Tobacco use—United States. 2. Tobacco habit—
United States. 3. Smoking—United States. I. Williams, Mary E.,
1960– . II. Series
HV5745.T44 2000
362.29'6'08350973—dc21
                                    99-27816
                                       CIP

©2000 by Greenhaven Press, Inc.
P.O. Box 289009, San Diego, CA 92198-9009

Printed in the U.S.A.

CONTENTS

FOREWORD

In the news, on the streets, and in neighborhoods, individuals are confronted with a variety of social problems. Such problems may affect people directly: A young woman may struggle with depression, suspect a friend of having bulimia, or watch a loved one battle cancer. And even the issues that do not directly affect her private life—such as religious cults, domestic violence, or legalized gambling—still impact the larger society in which she lives. Discovering and analyzing the complexities of issues that encompass communal and societal realms as well as the world of personal experience is a valuable educational goal in the modern world.

Effectively addressing social problems requires familiarity with a constantly changing stream of data. Becoming well informed about today's controversies is an intricate process that often involves reading myriad primary and secondary sources, analyzing political debates, weighing various experts' opinions—even listening to first-hand accounts of those directly affected by the issue. For students and general observers, this can be a daunting task because of the sheer volume of information available in books, periodicals, on the evening news, and on the Internet. Researching the consequences of legalized gambling, for example, might entail sifting through congressional testimony on gambling's societal effects, examining private studies on Indian gaming, perusing numerous websites devoted to Internet betting, and reading essays written by lottery winners as well as interviews with recovering compulsive gamblers. Obtaining valuable information can be time-consuming—since it often requires researchers to pore over numerous documents and commentaries before discovering a source relevant to their particular investigation.

Greenhaven's Contemporary Issues Companion series seeks to assist this process of research by providing readers with useful and pertinent information about today's complex issues. Each volume in this anthology series focuses on a topic of current interest, presenting informative and thought-provoking selections written from a wide variety of viewpoints. The readings selected by the editors include such diverse sources as personal accounts and case studies, pertinent factual and statistical articles, and relevant commentaries and overviews. This diversity of sources and views, found in every Contemporary Issues Companion, offers readers a broad perspective in one convenient volume.

In addition, each title in the Contemporary Issues Companion series is designed especially for young adults. The selections included in every volume are chosen for their accessibility and are expertly edited in consideration of both the reading and comprehension levels of the audience. The structure of the anthologies also enhances accessibility. An introductory essay places each issue in context and provides helpful facts such as historical background or current statistics and legislation that pertain to the topic. The chapters that follow organize the material and focus on specific aspects of the book's topic. Every essay is introduced by a brief summary of its main points and biographical information about the author. These summaries aid in comprehension and can also serve to direct readers to material of immediate interest and need. Finally, a comprehensive index allows readers to efficiently scan and locate content.

The Contemporary Issues Companion series is an ideal launching point for research on a particular topic. Each anthology in the series is composed of readings taken from an extensive gamut of resources, including periodicals, newspapers, books, government documents, the publications of private and public organizations, and Internet websites. In these volumes, readers will find factual support suitable for use in reports, debates, speeches, and research papers. The anthologies also facilitate further research, featuring a book and periodical bibliography and a list of organizations to contact for additional information.

A perfect resource for both students and the general reader, Greenhaven's Contemporary Issues Companion series is sure to be a valued source of current, readable information on social problems that interest young adults. It is the editors' hope that readers will find the Contemporary Issues Companion series useful as a starting point to formulate their own opinions about and answers to the complex issues of the present day.

Introduction

"There is a certain laid back vibe to smoking that we love," says Jamie Penn, a high school student who testified about teen smoking before a congressional panel. Moreover, he continues, "nothing combats emotional weariness like [the] feeling of reckless abandon [we get from] smoking." Indeed, inhaling cigarette smoke sets a number of processes in motion: The bloodstream immediately absorbs nicotine through the lungs; after about ten seconds, the nicotine reaches nerve-cell "nicotine receptors" in the brain, causing the secretion of a pleasure-inducing chemical, dopamine. Norepinephrine (which enhances energy and alertness) and endorphins (which causes relaxation and pain relief) are also released, creating the mental clarity and calmness that smokers relish. These pleasurable responses are one of the main reasons that many people become smokers. The habit of cigarette smoking, however, is dangerous. Regular smoking causes life-threatening cancers, cardiovascular disease, and emphysema. According to the U.S. Centers for Disease Control and Prevention (CDC), more people die each year from smoking-related diseases than the number of annual deaths caused by drug abuse, AIDS, traffic accidents, fires, murder, and suicide combined.

Moreover, the CDC reports, every day three thousand teenagers in the United States reach adulthood as habitual cigarette smokers. Most of these smokers had their first cigarette at age fourteen or fifteen; an estimated one out of four of them will die prematurely from smoking-related illnesses. Of the four hundred thousand adults who die each year of diseases caused by long-term tobacco use, the vast majority of them—more than 80 percent—began smoking cigarettes before the age of eighteen.

These statistics are of great concern to public health advocates. Although the overall number of U.S. smokers dropped during the last three decades of the twentieth century, this decline leveled off in the 1990s as a rise in the number of teens who begin to smoke each year made up for the number of adult smokers who quit or die. "Since the first Surgeon General's report [on the dangers of smoking] in 1964, the public health movement has been very successful in convincing adults not to start smoking," says John Pierce, an epidemiologist at the University of California in San Diego. "But we've had very little impact on kids."

Why do some teenagers start smoking? Many researchers, consumer advocates, and antismoking activists contend that tobacco industry marketing and promotion are largely responsible for the recent increase in youth smoking. Colorful cigarette ads are easily visible in mainstream magazines, on billboards, and next to cash registers in gas stations and convenience stores. Tobacco manufacturers often sponsor sporting events and concerts, where young people see cigarette logos featured near sports equipment and on posters and clothing. Nor are these promotional efforts the only media-related incentives for smoking. Films popular among teens often include main characters who smoke, such as Julia Roberts in *My Best Friend's Wedding,* Will Smith in *Independence Day,* and Leonardo DiCaprio in *Titanic.* University of Michigan survey researcher Lloyd D. Johnston maintains that through advertising and the media, "Smoking is continually associated with social success, sexual attractiveness, a healthy demeanor, exciting sporting activities, a cool and tough image for the boys, a slender body and liberated spirit for the girls, autonomy and independence for both sexes. What else could an American adolescent want?"

Many teen smokers, on the other hand, believe that media and advertising messages have little, if anything, to do with their decision to start smoking. Alex, a high school senior profiled in *Teens and Tobacco: A Fatal Attraction* by Susan Lang and Beth Marks, states that at age fourteen he started smoking because his friends smoked: "We were sitting around, and a few guys were smoking. A friend asked me to hold his cigarette, and I took a drag. I felt kind of dizzy and sick to my stomach, but I had two more that day. Then I kept doing it and doing it, and soon it became a habit." Tyler, a sixteen-year-old who participated in a discussion on teen smoking on National Public Radio's *Talk of the Nation,* says, "I [started smoking] mainly because it was my choice. Some of my friends smoked and some of them didn't . . . maybe I did it to tick my parents off or [as a] way of rebelling." Since nicotine can suppress appetite and speed up metabolism, some teens—particularly girls—smoke to control their weight, researchers maintain. Girls may also start smoking because it seems to help with the mood swings brought on by hormonal changes in puberty. As addiction psychiatrist Elizabeth Stuyt puts it, the drug nicotine tempers depression and anger: "It goes to the pleasure center of the brain and says, 'Chill out! Everything's going to be OK.'"

The primary factor affecting youth smoking, according to the R.J. Reynolds Tobacco Company, is the influence of peers and family. Many independent researchers grant that teens are more likely to smoke if their parents or friends smoke. Moreover, claims Lloyd Johnston, the number of teens who admit that they disapprove of smoking has declined since 1990, which means that today there is less peer pressure to abstain from smoking.

Most public health advocates, however, are not willing to let cigarette companies, the media, and advertisers off the hook. University of Illinois researcher Robin Mermelstein maintains that "kids are extraordinarily aware of the entertainment media. They are very reluctant to see the link between [media messages] and their behavior. But the influence is undoubtedly there." Antismoking groups often cite the success of the Joe Camel ad campaign as proof of the power of advertising aimed at youth. Joe Camel was the suave cartoon-character centerpiece of an R.J. Reynolds ad campaign that began in 1988. A 1991 study published by the *Journal of the American Medical Association* indicated that among six-year-olds, Joe Camel was as easily recognized as Mickey Mouse. Moreover, one year before the Joe Camel ad campaign began, Camel cigarettes had no share of the illegal youth market, but by 1995, Camels represented a 13.3 percent share of the adolescent cigarette market—leading many critics to argue that the ads were successfully attracting teens to the brand. These statistics drew such strong criticism from antismoking advocates that R.J. Reynolds discontinued the Joe Camel campaign in 1997.

As the result of a lawsuit that was settled in 1997, R.J. Reynolds was required to release to the public documents revealing that the company intentionally targeted teenagers in its marketing campaigns. For instance, a company memorandum from 1975 states: "[Camel filters] must increase its share penetration among the 14–24 age group, which have a new set of more liberal values and which represent tomorrow's cigarette business." R.J. Reynolds eventually planned to heavily advertise near video arcades, basketball courts, and other areas frequented by youths. Many consumer advocates see these and other similar documented decisions as definitive proof that cigarette manufacturers courted teen smokers and were fully aware of advertising's powerful effect on youths.

The pervasiveness of cigarette advertising and the rise in teen smoking were two of the high-profile issues addressed in tobacco legislation and litigation in the 1990s. Beginning in 1994, more than forty states sued the tobacco industry in an attempt to recover the health care costs of treating smoking-related illnesses. In response, the major cigarette manufacturers proposed a settlement in June 1997 in which they agreed to curb their marketing activities and initiate a campaign to reduce teen smoking in exchange for immunity from future lawsuits. Meanwhile, Republican senator John McCain drafted a congressional bill entitled the National Tobacco Policy and Youth Smoking Reduction Act. Designed to facilitate the creation of laws based on the proposed tobacco settlement, this bill also included several recommendations for reducing teen smoking: a tax increase on cigarettes, the banning of outdoor advertising and ads using cartoon, animal, or human figures, an end to cigarette vending machines, and a requirement that tobacco manufacturers lower the youth smoking rate by 60 percent over ten years. This bill, however, was rejected by the Senate in June 1998.

Although McCain's bill failed, in November 1998 the four largest tobacco companies and forty-six states agreed to a civil settlement loosely modeled on the original 1997 proposal. As part of this settlement, tobacco companies pledged to fund a $1.5 billion, five-year antismoking campaign that includes research and public education programs. In addition, cigarette manufacturers have agreed to certain marketing restrictions, including an end to the use of cartoon characters in ads, large-scale outdoor advertising, and the sale of logo-emblazoned merchandise. Moreover, tobacco labels can no longer sponsor most concerts, youth teams, and sporting events.

Public health advocates have mixed feelings about the tobacco settlement's potential to reduce youth smoking. Some antismoking groups are concerned about the loopholes in the agreement, which still allow significant amounts of advertising to reach teens. For example, each tobacco company can still sponsor one brand-name event each year, such as Brown and Williamson's Kool Jazz Festival. Cigarette companies can also promote their products within these annual events—including posters lauding the company's support and brand names painted on race cars. Outdoor advertising that emphasizes tobacco-company sponsorship is allowed ninety days before an annual event. Furthermore, cigarette manufacturers can use their corporate names—such as Philip Morris—to sponsor teams, athletes, musicians, and cultural events as long as such support does not include a domestic tobacco brand name. Cass Wheeler of the American Heart Association captured the public health community's sentiments regarding the tobacco settlement with these words: "Perfect? No. A beginning? Yes." Antismoking advocates hope to use the settlement as leverage for future tobacco legislation.

However, some analysts oppose further efforts to restrict tobacco advertising. Robert Levy, a senior fellow at the libertarian Cato Institute, argues that marketing constraints infringe on the tobacco industry's free-speech rights. According to Levy, the First Amendment bars any governmental interference with the tobacco industry's promotion of its product. In his opinion, the restrictions outlined in the now-defunct McCain bill would have been "an outrageous violation of the industry's right to advertise a legal product." Many of those who agree with Levy insist that the choice to start or to abstain from smoking can only be made by the individual, even if that individual is not yet an adult.

Others argue that restraints on tobacco advertising could actually backfire and lead to an increase in teen smoking. Since many youths start smoking to rebel against authority, these analysts contend that government curbs on tobacco advertising could increase the attraction of smoking for teenagers. Advertising restrictions in other countries have had mixed results, critics point out. In Finland, for example, partial bans on cigarette advertising went into effect in 1978. Although the incidence of male smoking did decrease from 35 percent to 27 percent by 1996, the number of women smokers remained the same, and the amount of Finnish teen smokers increased from 22 percent to 24 percent. Many public health groups assert that curbs on advertising will be ineffective without strongly enforced restrictions on youth access to cigarettes. Furthermore, these groups maintain, antismoking advocates must be observant and continually readjust their strategies until they discover the most effective ways to reduce youth smoking.

In the years to come, the issue of underage smoking is likely to draw continuing debate from scientists, politicians, educators, public health advocates, parents, and teenagers. *Teen Smoking: Contemporary Issues Companion* is an enlightening and engaging guide to this national controversy, with selections that provide historical background, health information, perspectives from smokers and ex-smokers, and a spectrum of opinion on the causes and effects of youth smoking.

CHAPTER 1

TEEN SMOKING AND THE WAR AGAINST TOBACCO

How the United States Became a Nation of Teen Smokers

Susan S. Lang and Beth H. Marks

Susan S. Lang and Beth H. Marks trace the history of U.S. tobacco consumption from precolonial times to the present. Tobacco was widely used by Native Americans before the arrival of Christopher Columbus, they point out, and eventually European explorers promoted its export around the world. Throughout the nineteenth and twentieth centuries, smoking was encouraged among U.S. soldiers—many of whom were teenagers—as cigarettes were said to provide comfort and boost morale. Aggressive advertising further helped to promote smoking among civilian adults and teens, Lang and Marks contend. In the late 1960s, however, the popularity of smoking decreased after scientists linked tobacco use to cancer and heart disease. Teen smoking remained in decline until 1980, the authors report, but since 1990 the percentage of underage smokers has increased. Lang is a senior science writer at Cornell University. Marks is a researcher, writer, and editor who lives in upstate New York.

We live in a country where about one-quarter of adults and up to 30 percent of teens finishing high school smoke cigarettes.

How did we get to a time and place where more than one out of four of us smoke despite smoking's hazards to our health? Over the centuries, has tobacco been a blessing or a curse? A pleasure or a poison? An asset or an affliction? How has this robust—but unspectacular—plant come to play such a major role in world commerce, social history, and human health? How did smoking become such a common habit?

This essay will trace tobacco's role and use through the ages to help us better understand how and why so many of us smoke cigarettes.

Tobacco and Native Americans

Tobacco (genus *Nicotiana*) belongs to the nightshade family of plants, which includes such diverse plants as potatoes, sweet peppers, petu-

Excerpted from *Teens and Tobacco: A Fatal Attraction*, by Susan S. Lang and Beth H. Marks. Copyright ©1996 by Susan S. Lang and Beth H. Marks. Used by permission of The Millbrook Press.

nias, and deadly nightshade. The species usually raised for cigarettes and cigars is *Nicotiana tabacum*. These plants may grow to be 4 to 6 feet high and bear huge rough and sticky leaves (8 to 14 inches wide and up to 20 inches long) that fan out from thick, strong stems topped with yellow or pink flowers.

Most experts believe that tobacco is native (grows naturally or wild) to the New World, what today is North and South America, including the United States. For centuries—from at least pre-Columbian times—these plants (*Nicotiana tabacum*) have flourished and have been cultivated in parts of South America, the Caribbean islands, and Central America. A more bitter variety *(N. rustica)* grew in Mexico and the eastern parts of North America. Still other small-leaved species grew west of the Andes and the Rocky Mountains.

For hundreds of years before the first European explorers set foot in the New World, native peoples smoked, chewed, and snuffed tobacco. According to Robert K. Heimann, author of *Tobacco and Americans*, the Caribs of the West Indies breathed or snuffed a tobacco mixture through a hollow Y-shaped tube called a "taboca" or "tobago," from which the word *tobacco* was probably derived. Natives of an island off Venezuela chewed tobacco "like cattle to such an extent that they could scarcely talk." The Mayans smoked, as did North American tribes who had access to only a bitter variety (*N. rustica*) and so smoked long pipes (war pipes, peace pipes, pleasure pipes, or calumets) to temper the harsh flavor of those leaves.

For some, tobacco was considered a medicine to ease childbirth pain, heal wounds, ward off hunger, or alleviate thirst (because it stimulates salivation). Many tribes viewed tobacco as sacred and included it in wedding, birth, death, and war rituals. Mayan priests believed its rising smoke carried messages to their gods. Others enjoyed tobacco for its smell. At different times, it also has been used as money or barter, as a measure of time (how long it took to smoke a pipe), and even as a way to induce hallucinations (when smoked and eaten in huge quantities).

But early accounts about tobacco also report that Native Americans smoked for its everyday pleasure. By the time the Europeans came to North America, Heimann reports, the tobacco plant was so widespread in the New World, and smoking, chewing, and snuffing so common, that "not one native culture in temperate and tropical North, Central and South America was found to lack some form of tobacco usage."

It was only a matter of time before the Europeans, after crossing the Atlantic, would also be lured by the appeal and pleasures of tobacco and smoking.

Tobacco and the Explorers

When Christopher Columbus and his Spanish crew (many of whom were just teenagers) arrived in the New World in 1492, they were showered with welcoming gifts from the natives. They relished the gifts of fruit and valued the wooden spears and other artifacts they received but threw out the dried and unfamiliar sweet-smelling leaves offered to them, thinking them worthless.

Some weeks later, however, the crew discovered a use for the leaves. Two of the crewmen, returning from a short scouting trip, reported having seen some Indians wrap the strange dried leaves "in the manner of a musket formed of paper," light one end, and breathe in smoke from the other. One of the two scouts, Rodrigo de Jerez, imitated what he had seen and became perhaps the first European tobacco smoker. When he later took his new habit home to Spain, priests there jailed him and denounced the smoke escaping from de Jerez's mouth as a sign of the devil. By the time de Jerez was released from prison a few years later, however, the tide had turned: many Europeans had taken up smoking.

In most of the New World, European adventurers (many young men still in their teens) in both South and North America encountered tobacco and brought it back home to Spain, Portugal, France, England, and Holland. Along with leaves, seeds, and tools for using the tobacco, many of these adventurers also brought home a well-established tobacco habit. And while traveling home, these early entrepreneurs left tobacco seeds in far-flung places—the Philippines, India, Polynesia—and maintained tobacco fields along the sea routes to ensure themselves a supply of tobacco on future voyages. It was these sailors—first explorers and later merchants—crisscrossing the Atlantic or rounding the Horn of Africa, bound for the East, who were most responsible for the rapid spread of tobacco throughout Europe, Asia, and Africa.

Tobacco and the Europeans

In Europe, tobacco quickly caught on. It was soon considered a holy herb, even a wonder drug, with marvelous curative powers, good for "a remedy for female problems, a snakebite antidote, lung strengthener, ulcer remedy, cure for the plague, and potent aphrodisiac," according to Beryl Brintnall Simpson and Molly Conner-Ororzaly, authors of *Economic Botany: Plants in Our World*. Jean Nicot de Villemain (after whom the words *nicotine* and the plant genus *Nicotiana* were named), the French ambassador to Portugal, boasted widely of tobacco's so-called medicinal value and reportedly sent the French court its first snuff in the mid–sixteenth century. By the late 1500s the European appetite for tobacco was so great that small tobacco fields throughout the world were expanded into plantations to supply the ever-increasing demand.

Yet tobacco also had its critics, particularly clergymen (men of the church) and doctors. Spanish priests condemned smoking as a deal made with the devil. Some doctors, contrary to those who believed

tobacco to be a cure-all, claimed that smoke filled the brain and blunt-
ed the senses. Others warned of sterility and birth defects. One English
doctor wrote: "Tobacco causes vomit and is an enemy of the stomach."

Some government leaders, believing tobacco to be evil, also tried to
curb tobacco use. One Russian czar ordered that nostrils of snuffers be
split so they couldn't indulge their habit; another czar ordered smokers whipped for their first offense, killed for a second. A Chinese
emperor had tobacco importers beheaded, while a Turkish sultan executed as many as eighteen smokers a day!

Instead of abusing smokers or snuffers, some rulers tried to discourage tobacco use in other ways. King James I of England was an ardent
tobacco opponent; in 1604 he denounced smoking as "loathsome,"
"hateful," and "dangerous to the lungs." To control his countrymen's
appetite for tobacco, James I limited tobacco imports. The resulting
reduced supply simply fanned demand and pushed prices higher. At
one point, a pound of tobacco was worth more than a pound of sil-
ver! James responded by boosting his tobacco tax 4,000 percent,
assuming the huge duty would further curb imports. This tactic also
backfired. Smugglers grew rich, farmers grew tobacco . . . and more
people than ever smoked.

James I eventually admitted defeat in his crusade against the "pre-
cious stink" and turned England's tobacco cravings to his advantage:
the government took control of importing and selling tobacco, with
revenues going into the national treasury. France, Italy, Russia, and
Prussia soon followed suit. The governments grew richer on tobacco
while the consciences of those who opposed tobacco use on moral or
medical grounds were eased by the high taxes—today we refer to such
taxes as "sin taxes."

Tobacco and American Colonists

By 1620 tobacco was a booming commercial crop in the American
colonies; by the end of the century an acre of tobacco was worth four
times an acre of corn. Huge tobacco plantations, manned by thousands of slaves, dotted the Eastern Seaboard, especially in the Chesa-
peake tidewater region of Virginia and Maryland. By 1698 Virginia
and Maryland together were exporting more than twenty-three million pounds of tobacco a year to Europe.

Although colonial Americans used tobacco themselves, almost the
entire tobacco crop was exported at that time. Pipes and snuff grew
increasingly popular in the 1700s, mimicking habits abroad, and were
viewed as a "creature comfort." To keep up the morale of his Revolu-
tionary troops, George Washington, commander in chief of the
armies and himself a successful tobacco planter, begged for aid for his
soldiers: "I say, if you can't send money, send tobacco."

Just as tobacco use kept climbing elsewhere in the world, it did in
the young United States. By the 1790s chewing tobacco became more

stylish than the pipes and snuff of colonial times. Tobacco chewing was regarded as down-to-earth, a habit for "real men," both urban and rural. Chaw was practical and portable; no pipe, flame, or snuff-box was needed—just a place to spit!

Congressmen, particularly during Andrew Jackson's presidency (1829–1837), chewed tobacco as a way of linking themselves with the common folk they represented. The British novelist Charles Dickens, on a U.S. tour, was appalled by this nation's filthy habit:

> Washington may be called the headquarters of tobacco-tinctured saliva. In all the public places of America, this filthy custom is recognized. In the courts of law, the judge has his spittoon, the crier his, the witness his, and the prisoner his.

By 1860 America's tobacco appetite equaled the amount shipped abroad. Cigars grew in popularity, and by 1870 Americans (mostly males) smoked 1.2 billion cigars and used another 100 million pounds of tobacco in pipes, chewing tobacco, or snuff. That's 60 cigars and 5 pounds of other tobacco used for every American male (from infants on up!) that year. Ten years later the figures had more than doubled: 2.75 billion cigars and 200 million pounds of pipe and chewing tobacco plus snuff were consumed in 1880.

The use of tobacco continued to climb, fueled by a new, cheap smoke . . . the cigarette.

The Influx of Cigarettes

Native Americans smoked cigars (rolled tobacco leaves cemented with spit) and also made cigarettes ("small cigars") from tobacco scraps and waste. These early cigarettes caught on, according to one historian, with "lower-class people, members of the lesser breeds, and inferior individuals—which translated into children, the poor, and women."

European cigarettes had a similar history. In the 1500s poor people often sifted through garbage to salvage cigar butts, partially burned pipe tobacco, and snuff dust. They mixed these tidbits together, rolled them in scrap paper, and puffed away—an inspired recycling effort that resulted in cheap (or free) smokes. A lower-class pleasure in Paris and London, cigarette smoking was later adopted by bohemians (artists, writers, revolutionaries) in many European cities.

During the Crimean War (1853–1856; a conflict in which Britain and France joined Turkey in its fight against Russia), however, the cigarette habit spread across classes and nations. Soldiers (again, many were teenagers) traded tobacco and picked up the habit, in an attempt to escape from the anxiety and boredom of war. As in future wars, tobacco use rose when soldiers brought their new habit home after the war.

In the United States, it was the Civil War that spread the cigarette habit. Many soldiers took up smoking as a cheap, convenient way of

consuming tobacco. After the war, soldiers introduced friends to cigarettes. Cigars were still the gentleman's smoke, but more and more
ordinary people began smoking cigarettes as a low-cost alternative.

By the 1880s high-speed machines for mass-producing cigarettes
were vastly increasing cigarette production. In 1890 per capita (how
much per person, including children, in the nation) consumption
rose to 35 cigarettes each. In 1910 the figure was 85, and by 1930 it
had skyrocketed to almost 1,000!

War was to spread cigarettes once again even deeper into American
culture. During World War I (1914–1918), an army doctor reported
that the cigarette "is an indispensable comfort to the men." General
John J. Pershing, head of the U.S. Army in Europe, cabled home:
"Tobacco is as indispensable as the daily ration; we must have thousands of tons of it without delay." At another time, Pershing said,
"You ask me what we need to win this war. I answer tobacco as much
as bullets." During these times, according to Robert Sobel, author of
They Satisfy: The Cigarette in American Life, cigarettes "came to be identified with all the positive values—quiet dignity, courage, and dedica-
tion above all."

World War II (1939–1945) had much the same effect on spreading
the smoking habit. Most soldiers, sailors, and pilots (many of whom
were in their teens) smoked with gusto, and Americans at home followed suit. Cigarettes were again deemed essential to the morale of
the troops and were included in field rations (along with dehydrated
soup, lemonade mix, and Spam). President Franklin D. Roosevelt classified tobacco as an essential crop and required draft boards to give
deferments to tobacco farmers to ensure maximum production. By
the end of the war, cigarette sales were higher than ever before. Billboards, radios, movies, magazines, and newspapers carried engaging
cigarette ads with catchy jingles. By 1947 per capita cigarette consumption in the United States was 128 packs of cigarettes smoked for
every man, woman, and child! Three out of every four men smoked
cigarettes; half that number of women smoked; teenagers smoked.
America was hooked.

Anti-Cigarette Efforts

As cigarettes grew more popular, opponents grew more vocal. The early anti-tobacco movement, led by educators and reformers, rallied to
protect the nation's youth (specifically boys) from the evils of smoking. By 1890 twenty-six states had passed laws prohibiting the sale of
cigarettes to minors. Few, however, paid much attention to the laws,
which were difficult to enforce.

But one reformer, Lucy Page Gaston, believed that smoking led to
drink, disease, crime, and death; she founded the Chicago Anti-Cigarette League in 1899. Among other activities, the league hired officers
to arrest anyone younger than eighteen seen smoking in public and

tried to prohibit the sale of cigarettes as the only sure way to keep cigarettes away from youth.

Others also spoke out about the destructive influence of cigarettes on youth, saying that smoking lowered intelligence, school performance, and lung capacity and promoted insomnia, high blood pressure, and bronchial problems. Moral arguments were also offered. The president of the New York City Board of Education said that "cigarette fiends" in public schools stole money for smokes, and concluded that the "cigarette habit is more devastating to the health and morals of young men than any habit or vice that can be named." Cigarettes were also blamed for rising juvenile crime rates.

The anti-cigarette efforts worked, but only briefly. By 1909 fifteen states banned cigarette sales completely, yet cigarette use kept climbing. The laws were eventually repealed. To make cigarettes even more attractive, tobacco companies launched an aggressive advertising campaign showing cigarettes as a symbol of youth and beauty. Soon middle-class women and teenagers were taking up the habit as never before.

By 1952, 800,000 teenagers were picking up the habit every year. At the same time, however, researchers were slowly but surely linking cigarette smoking with lung cancer, heart disease, and other serious health problems.

Smoking, Health, and Today's Smoking Patterns

By the early 1960s researchers had substantial evidence that cigarette smoking was linked to lung cancer and an overall higher death rate. One study of men between the ages of forty-five and sixty-four, for example, found that death rates of smokers were twice as high as those of nonsmokers, while death rates from lung cancer among smokers were ten times higher! These rates were confirmed by a study of more than one million American adults conducted in the 1960s: 1,385 smokers died during the study, compared to 662 nonsmokers. Of the smokers, 110 had died from lung cancer, compared with only 12 deaths among nonsmokers. More than twice as many smokers (654) died of coronary heart disease than did nonsmokers (304). Differences in numbers of deaths due to emphysema and various cancers (mouth, pharynx, larynx, esophagus, pancreas, and bladder) were also striking.

In 1961 representatives from major American health organizations urged President John F. Kennedy to do something about the tobacco problem. He responded by forming the Surgeon General's Advisory Committee on Smoking and Health. In 1964 the committee published its report, *Smoking and Health*. The conclusions were sobering: cigarette smoking is a major cause of lung cancer; smokers are nine or ten times more likely to get lung cancer than are nonsmokers; the more a person smokes, the greater are his chances of contracting lung cancer; smoking also contributes to heart disease, bronchitis, and emphysema.

At first Americans took the report to heart. Cigarette sales declined 20 percent within two months. But habit and heavy advertising led to a rebound—cigarette sales in 1965 were 562 billion, the highest ever.

In 1966 cigarette packages were required by law to carry a health-hazard warning. By 1971 cigarette advertising was banned from television and radio.

Gradually Americans began to heed the health warnings and give up cigarettes. Smokers declined from 40 percent of the adult population in 1965 to almost 26 percent in 1991, and the percentage has held steady since then.

Today about 46 million—about one-quarter—of American adults smoke cigarettes; 44 million have kicked the habit. In fact, among American males today, there are more former smokers than current smokers. Even current smokers have gotten the message: four out of every five adult smokers say they would like to quit. Unfortunately, teens have not followed the same trend.

Smoking and Teens

Historically, male teens have come of age as adults much earlier than they do today. As adult smoking caught on, so did teen smoking. By age sixteen or seventeen, teen boys were considered adult, old enough to marry and fight in wars. The trends we've discussed historically have included these older teens.

In the twentieth century, however, teens have been more separate from adults, not coming of age until their late teens or even early twenties. In the late 1960s and early 1970s the baby boomers (the generation born after World War II), then teenagers, began to smoke. In fact, they smoked more cigarettes per day than did their parents. In 1976 about 38 percent of high-school seniors reported regular smoking (within the past thirty days), and approximately 28 percent were daily smokers. Most were light smokers (half a pack per day or less); only 3 percent smoked more than a pack per day.

As medical evidence against cigarettes mounted, the rate of youth smoking dropped until 1980, when it leveled off. In 1980 about 30 percent of high-school seniors were regular smokers and 21 percent were daily smokers.

Although these figures remained steady for more than a decade, teen smoking has been climbing recently. For example, the number of eighth graders who smoke at least once a month jumped 30 percent between 1991 and 1994. In 1994 one out of every five eighth graders and one out of every three twelfth graders smoked cigarettes.

WHY SMOKING IS A REAL DRAG

Debi Martin-Morris

In the following selection, freelance writer and reporter Debi Martin-Morris discusses the dangerous effects of cigarettes and the reasons why some teens start smoking. According to Martin-Morris, many young women start smoking due to peer pressure and because the calming effects of nicotine help them deal with the mood swings caused by adolescent hormonal changes. Once teenagers start smoking, however, they often become addicted and prone to cancer, emphysema, and heart disease in adulthood, the author warns.

Lauren Kramer had been stood up by her best friend on a Saturday night. "We had this huge fight on the phone," says Lauren, a 17-year-old from Queens, N.Y. "She was supposed to be spending the night at my house, but instead she was hanging with these other people."

Lauren was pissed. She slammed the phone down, headed out the front door, sat on the front porch steps—and lit a cigarette. "It calms me down and helps me think," Lauren says of her smoking habit. "After I had a cigarette, I was able to go back inside, call my friend and work everything out. If I hadn't had one, I probably would have called her back and yelled and screamed, and it would have been a horrible night. Having a cigarette helps me control my emotions. My problems are still there, but the tension is gone."

So a cigarette saved Lauren's Saturday night. But at what price? Addiction to a drug that can cause cancer and heart disease. In other words, kills.

Smoking-Coping Syndrome

The National Institute on Drug Abuse (NIDA) says nicotine, the psychoactive drug in cigarettes, affects brain chemistry, acting as both stimulant and sedative to the central nervous system. It increases concentration and alters mood. And it "works" fast: A puff of nicotine reaches the brain in seconds.

People who smoke may not care about the scientific stuff—like Lauren, they simply instinctively sense that they think more clearly after lighting up. That's how they get hooked. Life is full of problems,

Reprinted, with permission, from "Why Smoking's a Real Drag!" by Debi Martin-Morris, *Teen*, January 1998.

and if cigarettes become part of the coping process, grabbing a smoke to deal becomes an everyday (or every other minute!) occurrence, explains Ann E. Schensky, the director of the youth education program for the Center for Tobacco Research and Intervention (CTRI) at the University of Wisconsin Medical School in Madison.

That's a real drag, since cigarette smoke is composed of a dozen gases (mainly carbon monoxide), nicotine and tar. The tar exposes smokers to high rates of lung cancer, emphysema and bronchial diseases, and carbon monoxide increases the chances of cardiovascular diseases. NIDA, the U.S. Surgeon General and the American Medical Association have all determined that the nicotine in cigarettes is as psychologically and physically addictive as heroin, cocaine and alcohol.

Scary. Even scarier are these smoking statistics:

• According to the Surgeon General and the Food and Drug Administration (FDA), 3,000 children and adolescents become regular smokers every day, and nearly 1,000 will die prematurely from smoking-related diseases.

• An estimated 4.5 million children and teens smoke in the United States, according to the Centers for Disease Control (CDC).

• Eighty-nine percent of all persons who ever try a cigarette do so by age 18; of those who smoke daily, 71 percent had smoked daily by age 18, says the CDC. The younger people start smoking, the more likely they are to become addicted to nicotine.

• More than 400,000 people die per year from smoking-related diseases, more than those who die from car wrecks, alcohol, drugs, sexually transmitted diseases and homicide combined, says the CDC.

All the Wrong Reasons

Nicotine dependency is the most common form of drug addiction and causes more deaths and disease than all other addictions combined, reports the CDC. And when it comes to addictive behaviors, cigarette smoking is the one most likely to take hold during adolescence. So with all those people smoking, there have to be other "reasons" for it beyond being a coping mechanism.

And there are—especially if you ask young women. Some start smoking because it's still considered cool in certain circles (cigarette advertising sure tries to make it seem that way!). Peer pressure is really powerful, and if the popular crowd says, "If you light up, you're down," that can be hard to resist.

Another draw for girls who start smoking during puberty is it seems to help with hormonal changes that cause mood fluctuations. "Nicotine works like other drugs when it comes to anger, depression and mood swings," says Elizabeth Stuyt, M.D., who runs a support group and specializes in addiction psychiatry at Lubbock's Texas Tech University Health Sciences Center. "It goes to the pleasure center of the brain and says, 'Chill out! Everything's going to be OK.'"

Then there are the numerous studies that show nicotine speeds up metabolism and suppresses appetite—a big issue with girls concerned about their weight. Most teenage girls, once they start smoking regularly, may gain weight when they quit. Research also shows that quitting smoking without changing eating or exercise habits results in weight gain, regardless of age. "I don't want to gain 10 pounds and most of the teenage girls I work with don't either," says Schensky.

Quit or Miss

About two-thirds of adolescent smokers say they want to quit, and 70 percent say they wouldn't have started if they could choose again. Trouble is, smoking is an addiction and kicking the habit can be as hard as quitting heroin, cocaine or alcohol, according to NIDA.

"I feel trapped," says Lauren, who's tried unsuccessfully to quit several times. Since first lighting up at age 11, Lauren hasn't been able to stop for more than a month. She smokes before and after school on weekdays, and on weekends inhales a pack a day and often chain smokes.

It's not that Lauren's surrounded by smokers at home who don't care about her (or their own) health; in fact, her mother is an associate director of the American Lung Association in New York! "I tell her about the people I know who died of lung cancer," says her mom, Joanne Kramer. "I bring posters and brochures home. I say to her, 'Who would want to kiss you, Ashtray Breath?' If I see her smoking, I grab the cigarette; if I find a pack, I throw it out. Once I made her smoke a half a pack of cigarettes, one after another, until she threw up. That didn't work. It's really sad, considering my job is to increase public awareness about the dangers of cigarettes and I can't even get my own kid to quit."

"It gets harder to quit the older you get," says Susan Kleir, a 20-year-old college student from Chicago who started smoking at 14. "I don't actually enjoy it anymore. I smoke because I can't stand the way I feel when I don't smoke—it's PMS times 10."

Alisa Flaum, 23, says she'd quit, "if I didn't think I'd go insane. There are so many things in my daily life I don't know how to do without a cigarette. I've never driven a car without a cigarette. I've never worked at my computer without a cigarette."

Quitting isn't easy, but it can be done. Getting off nicotine should be gradual, so withdrawal symptoms are less severe and relapse is less likely. The optimal treatment combines counseling and support groups with nicotine replacement medications such as nicotine chewing gum or the transdermal patch, both of which wean smokers off nicotine.

Joe Camel's Walking Papers

Reducing teen smoking is a Clinton administration priority. The idea is to make it difficult for young people to get cigarettes. In February 1997 it became unlawful for cigarettes to be sold to anyone under age

18. Already, a pack-a-day habit is costly, not only physically but financially. With the average price of a pack of cigarettes hovering around $2 in most states, a pack-a-day habit can cost $732 a year and $7,320 over 10 years. And President Bill Clinton has proposed increasing the price of a pack of cigarettes by $1.50 over the next 10 years!

Clinton and Congress continue to debate whether the FDA will be given the authority to regulate nicotine as an addictive drug, which might change the way cigarettes are made and distributed, making it even harder for teens to buy them.

The issue of teen smoking is big at the state and local government level too. In parts of California, Florida, Texas and Illinois, for example, fines ranging from $25 to $250 may be doled out to convicted underage smokers. Other penalties can include driver's license suspension, community service and/or attendance at a tobacco-awareness class.

Another controversial tactic being discussed is the banning of all cigarette advertising that teens might see. "There's little doubt that advertising geared toward teens is a prominent factor," says CTRI's Schensky. "It's no wonder the three most popular brands with teens are the most advertised ones."

Those who support banning cigarette advertising point to a study that found 6-year-olds to be as familiar with Joe Camel as they were with Mickey Mouse. (Joe Camel's employers have already decided not to use the cartoon figure in any future campaigns.) But banning cigarette ads will not by itself keep teens from smoking. "Every semester I ask my students to raise their hands if they smoke—lots of hands go up," says Frances L. Collins, an assistant professor of advertising at Kent State University in Ohio. "Then I ask how many smoke because of cigarette advertising. No hands go up. They laugh. That's hardly a scientific sample, but the idea that kids smoke because they see a colorful cartoon character is like saying kids speak in a high, squeaky voice because Mickey Mouse does."

Alisa agrees. "Joe Camel looking cool has no effect on me," she says. "I'm completely indifferent to the Marlboro man." So what did get her started? Alisa can't put her finger on any single factor: For her, smoking was a social thing—and that's the way it begins for lots of girls. "Most teenage girls who experiment with alcohol or marijuana don't do it all the time, but the girls I work with are likely to smoke all day, every day," says Stuyt. "They don't even know they're addicted—until they try to quit."

Just ask Alisa. "I'm a full-fledged nicotine addict. I have asthma, my father is a physician . . . yet I can't stop. It defies all rationality—it's just crazy. I really wish I'd never started."

BLACK LUNGS: AFRICAN AMERICAN TEENS AND SMOKING

Salim Muwakkil

Salim Muwakkil examines the recent rise in popularity of cigarettes among African American teens—a trend that reverses several previous years of decreasing rates of smoking among black
youth. The author attributes this new trend to the tobacco
industry's intentional targeting of young blacks as a market. This
situation is further complicated, the author maintains, by the
fact that the black media and major civil rights organizations are
largely sponsored and underwritten by cigarette manufacturers.
African Americans must take decisive action to save black youth
from tobacco addiction, he concludes. Muwakkil is a senior editor of *In These Times*, a biweekly progressive journal.

In 1994, cigarette makers attempted to parlay black youth's fascina-
tion with the martyred Malcolm X into big profits. In the wake of
Spike Lee's brilliant marketing campaign for his movie *Malcolm X*,
T-shirts and baseball caps bearing an "X" logo were omnipresent in
the black community. So Star Tobacco Corporation began to manufac-
ture a menthol cigarette called "X." Packaged in the red, black and
green colors of the black nationalist movement, the cigarettes were
marketed in 20 states before a coalition of outraged African-American
community groups successfully forced the manufacturers to discontinue the brand.

Anti-tobacco activists successfully beat back this and a few other
clumsy attempts to push nicotine to black teens. But the cigarette
industry has had the last laugh. A recently released study by the Centers for Disease Control and Prevention (CDC) found that the consistent decline in smoking once seen among African-American youth
has reversed dramatically. While a 1991 poll found that only 12.6 percent of African-American high school students admitted to smoking
cigarettes in the past month, that number jumped to 22.7 percent in
1997. That's an 80 percent increase in just six years.

There are several reasons why this has happened. The most obvious
is the marketing savvy employed by the tobacco companies, especial-

Reprinted from "Black Lungs," by Salim Muwakkil, *In These Times*, June
14, 1998, by permission of *In These Times*, a Chicago-based newsmagazine,
www.inthesetimes.com.

ly when targeting black youth. But the credibility cigarette makers gained by supporting black organizations and the tobacco industry's heavy advertising presence in black publications also has had an impact. And a trend among black youth of mixing tobacco with marijuana has probably worsened the problem. With smoking the leading preventable cause of death in the United States—and with 50,000 African-Americans dying of smoking-related illnesses every year—these new trends are a cause for alarm.

The sharp increase in smoking rates among black teens during the past few years is particularly disturbing because for many years smoking rates among young blacks had been going down—a major victory, since as a whole African-Americans are still more likely to smoke than any ethnic group except Native Americans. "In 1976, there was no difference between blacks and whites," says Michael Ericksen, director of the CDC's office on smoking and health. "Then there was this huge divergence, and black youth began to view smoking as a 'white thing.' Now it has turned around, and we don't know what happened."

Rep. John Conyers (D-Mich.) thinks he knows: The tobacco industry sped up its efforts to hook young blacks. In February 1998, he released a list of documents to support his claim. Among them was a 1973 document from the Brown & Williamson Tobacco Corporation showing that the bulk of sales increases in the company's Kool brand was among 16- to 25-year-olds, a demographic that would "soon be three times as important to Kool." A Lorillard Tobacco research study noted that in 1978 the success of its Newport brand was largely due to black high school students.

Although these documents are now two decades old, they help establish the context for what's going on now. As National Medical Association (NMA) president Nathaniel Murdock told the House Subcommittee on Health and the Environment in testimony in March 1998, "Recently released documents related to the deliberate practices to capture African-American smokers do not present the entire picture as to how the tobacco industry promoted and continues to promote nicotine addiction."

Targeting Young Blacks

The NMA, the country's largest organization of black physicians, and other anti-tobacco groups argue that the industry should be required to fully disclose how it targeted African-Americans. It charges that, among other things, the billboard advertisements currently saturating black communities are specifically aimed at minority youth.

The Summit Health Coalition, a national network of organizations focused on African-American health issues, notes that 20 percent of the advertising budget for Kool cigarettes was dedicated to marketing targeted at African-Americans, although blacks represent just 12 percent of the population. The group charges that young minorities have been targeted more aggressively as general levels of smoking have declined. Murdock suggests that the tobacco industry should be made accountable for the inordinate number of deaths in the African-American community due to smoking. "They should also donate to the traditional black medical schools for further research and prevention of cancer of the lungs and other related diseases," he says.

But some anti-smoking activists don't think the tobacco companies are the only people to blame. In fact, some are scathingly critical of major black institutions for their role in pushing—or at least condoning—nicotine addiction. Black newspapers, for example, have had a long, cooperative and profitable relationship with the tobacco industry. Cigarette manufacturers were among the first businesses to advertise in black publications, according to Robert Bogle, publisher of the *Philadelphia Tribune* and former president of the National Newspaper Publishers Association (NNPA), a trade group representing 250 black-owned papers.

When evidence of smoking's health dangers began surfacing, though, black newspapers were conspicuously silent. And as the tobacco industry came under increasing attack by anti-smoking activists, it found a safe haven in many black newspapers. Seldom were anti-smoking articles published in NNPA newspapers. "Tobacco companies were our friends before anybody else was," says Bogle. "A lot of groups have condemned us for taking those ads, but for many of our newspapers it was a matter of economic survival. And as long as it's legal to grow it and smoke it, why should we be left out?"

Tobacco ads now represent 60 percent of ad space for most black newspapers, according to current NNPA President Dorothy Leavell. "Tobacco ads influence us," she says. "We've pretty much taken the position that people should have the freedom to make their own decision about whether or not they want to smoke."

Tobacco Industry Sponsorship

The tobacco industry also markets its product by underwriting events in the black community and by helping to sponsor conventions of the major civil rights organizations, including the National Urban League, the National Association for the Advancement of Colored People and the Rainbow/PUSH Coalition. The College Fund (formerly the United Negro College Fund) is a recipient of some of the tobacco companies' most generous grants. The Congressional Black Caucus Foundation receives thousands in tobacco cash. Cultural organizations, including the Dance Theater of Harlem and the National Black Arts Festival, regularly receive generous donations from the industry. The Kool Jazz Festival, which travels across the country during the summer, is a salient example of tobacco marketers' pervasive presence in the black community.

Civil rights groups are attempting to distance themselves from tobacco money, but that's no easy task. In the past, these groups have justified their indulgence by arguing that tobacco companies are attempting to balance the harm they do with the money they give. Few still make that argument. "We're trying to wean ourselves away from this source of revenue," Hugh Price, president of the National Urban League, recently told the Chicago radio station WVON. "And, quite frankly, it's not easy. Without additional sources [of income], we have to scale back on some of our important projects."

Still, tobacco is so ingrained into black life that few African-American leaders express appropriate concern, complains Makani Themba, co-director of the Oakland-based Praxis Project, which targets tobacco marketing. Tobacco companies fund African-American music, art, concerts, schools and churches. They give money to African-American family reunion groups and sponsor family reunion storytelling contests for children. What's perhaps most tragic is that streets in African-American communities are full of larger-than-life images glamorizing these deadly products.

Another part of the problem is black youth smoking marijuana in hollowed-out cigars, or "blunts." The practice is said to have started in Jamaica, where marijuana is routinely mixed with tobacco, and it took hold in New York City in the mid-'80s. Health experts worry that this new trend has provoked a "reverse gateway" effect, bringing marijuana smokers to tobacco rather than vice versa. Although cigar makers like Havatampa (makers of the popular Phillies Blunts) deny that they intentionally exploit this clandestine trend critics are not so sure. "I see ads for Phillies Blunts in some stores in Philadelphia that clearly seem to be capitalizing on the kids' blunts craze," says Charyn Sutton, co-founder of the National Association of African-Americans for Positive Imagery.

Anti-Tobacco Efforts

A few groups of African-Americans are fighting tobacco advertising. Several anti-tobacco groups have started "white out" campaigns, defacing billboards that glamorize smoking. And Conyers is working within the legal system to make black concerns a vital part of tobacco negotiations in Washington. [In June 1998, a comprehensive federal anti-smoking bill failed in the U.S. Senate. However, in a November 1998 civil settlement, the nation's biggest tobacco companies agreed to pay 46 states $206 billion and to submit to marketing and advertising restrictions. As of March 1999, a federal lawsuit was pending.] Since we know part of the blame lies squarely at the feet of the tobacco industry, argues Conyers, "there is compelling need for blacks to be included in the settlement talks." The settlement . . . addresses a variety of issues—including the Food and Drug Administration's authority to regulate tobacco advertising and promotion, and youth access to tobacco products—in exchange for giving the tobacco industry immunity from future lawsuits. But it didn't acknowledge the tobacco industry's special efforts to induce African-Americans to smoke.

It's important for black America's public health that the settlement do so. For instance, industry-paid public service announcements about the dangers of smoking will likely be part of any deal. But most current anti-smoking campaigns don't speak to African-American children's cultural reality. And since the "blunt" trend is in part fueling this new spurt of tobacco use, anti-smoking messages should forthrightly confront the practice.

Pushing nicotine is drug dealing of the most lethal kind. Tobacco is so addictive that it has become deeply insinuated into American culture. But this culturally sanctioned pushing has become too deadly to tolerate, and African-Americans, who have been especially victimized, are finally jumping into the front ranks of the anti-tobacco movement. It's about time.

THE DANGERS OF SMOKING ARE EXAGGERATED

Rosalind B. Marimont

In the following selection, Rosalind B. Marimont argues that the dangers of smoking have been grossly overstated. She points out, for example, that statistical flaws and erroneous computer applications caused the Centers for Disease Control and Prevention to overestimate the number of annual deaths resulting from smoking. Marimont contends that this faulty information about smoking has distorted the nation's health priorities for teenagers—a group that faces much more danger from alcohol and drugs than from cigarettes. Marimont is a retired mathematician and scientist who is active in health policy issues.

That smoking causes 400,000 deaths annually is now widely promoted as a statistical truth. The recent campaign against teenage smoking asserted that one out of three teenagers who smoked would be killed by his habit. These numbers are a gross misinterpretation of the Centers for Disease Control (CDC) SAMMEC results, and a gross overestimate of the importance of smoking as a cause of death. [SAMMEC stands for Smoking-Attributable Mortality, Morbidity, and Economic Cost, a computer program developed by the CDC.] Another mantra of the Anti-Smoking Partisans (ASPs) is that smoking kills more people than alcohol and drugs combined. This latter piece of disinformation has been used to justify neglect of the shocking rise in teenage binge drinking and driving. In 1996, neither candidate for president even mentioned teenage drinking, and the Clintons hardly mentioned drugs until the Republicans made an issue of it.

A Lack of Scientific Integrity

The 400,000 plus estimate is the result of logical and epidemiological blunders and a lack of scientific integrity by the fanatic anti-smoking lobby. The CDC estimate is described as the number of deaths *associated* with smoking, not *caused by* it. This is not a semantic distinction, because a death can be associated with many factors.

Among risk factors for heart disease, for example, are hypertension,

Reprinted, with permission, from "The Blunders of SAMMEC: 400,000 Killed by Smoking!?" by Rosalind B. Marimont, published at www.forces.org/articles/files/sammec.htm.

high serum cholesterol, obesity, sedentary life style, smoking, and genetic factors. If we ran SAMMEC computations for each of these factors, we could estimate the number of heart disease deaths associated with each one. But suppose that John Smith, who died of heart disease, had all of these factors. He would have contributed 6 deaths to the total associated deaths. So that when we sum up these results to arrive at the total deaths, we find that our total is *much larger than the number of people who actually died of heart disease.*

A simple numerical example will demonstrate the SAMMEC method, and its multiple counting error. Let us consider heart disease. A behavior or attribute is said to be a risk factor for death by heart disease (HD) if the population exhibiting that behavior has a higher HD mortality rate than the population which does not exhibit that behavior. If obese people have a higher mortality rate than non-obese, obesity is a risk factor for heart disease death. The ratio of these two mortality rates is unknown as the risk ratio of obesity for heart disease death, and of course, is measured statistically.

How does SAMMEC compute the deaths associated with some risk ratio? Assume that we have measured the risk ratio of obesity for HD death to be 4. Assume that we have a population of 1000 people, of whom 500 are obese and 500 are not. We observe 10 deaths by heart disease. We can then compute that 8 of these deaths would occur among the obese, and 2 among the non-obese, the ratio of 4:1. Let us call this risk ratio r. Then SAMMEC assumes that if the obese people were not obese, they would have the same mortality rate as the non-obese, or only 2 deaths. Therefore 6 deaths among the obese are attributed to obesity, or the fraction (1-⅟ᵣ) of the deaths of the obese, in this case ¾. It is easy to compute the fraction of the total deaths, which is called *the SAF, or statistically attributable factor. If we stopped at this point, we would say that obesity causes ¾ of the deaths of all obese heart disease patients.*

A Statistical Overcount

But is this true? Let us continue our computation, and consider hypertension as a risk factor for HD death. To simplify the calculations let us assume that hypertension also has a risk ratio of 4, and this is the crux of the overcount, assume that the same group of people who are obese are also the hypertensives. Then we find that 6 deaths of our hypertensive group are attributed to hypertension. Similarly we can find that smoking, lack of exercise, and high cholesterol levels each result in 6 deaths. So that we find that our 5 risk factors are associated with 30 deaths by heart disease. *But only 10 people died altogether, and only 8 in the high risk group.* Only if each person had only 1 risk factor for any cause of death would the SAMMEC SAF be a true fraction, in the sense that all fractions would add up to 1.

This overcount is not the only problem with the SAMMEC system.

In estimating risk ratios, we compared death rates of smokers to those of non-smokers. This ratio would be a true estimate of the effects of smoking only if the two groups were identical in all other respects than smoking. This of course is not true—the measurement is done without controls. For this reason epidemiologists rarely take seriously risk ratios of less than 3.

In the SAMMEC report, of 102 risk ratios of smoking for various diseases, only 40 are greater than 3. *If we consider only risk ratios* equal to or greater than 3, *the number of deaths is cut in half, to about 200,000.* Even if we reject only those less than 2, the number is cut by about one third, to about 270,000. And these corrections still leave a number of serious confounders.

One of the most serious confounders in smoking studies is the inverse correlation of smoking with socio-economic status (SES). Low SES is one of the best predictors of disease and early death.

Benefits of Smoking

And finally, no attention is paid to the benefits of smoking. For some conditions, such as obesity, the risk ratio of smoking is less than 1, since smokers are less likely than non-smokers to be obese. Also, smokers are less likely to have ulcerative colitis. It is of course heresy to suggest that smoking can have any good effects, but like caffeine, nicotine is known to improve alertness, and allay depression and anxiety. There is recent evidence that smoking may provide some protection against Alzheimer's disease and Parkinson's. These good effects are rarely mentioned for fear of being branded a tool of the tobacco companies.

It has been said that truth is the first casualty of war. The deceptions of the war on smoking have done incalculable harm to the nation. The grossly overstated dangers of smoking to health have distorted the nation's health priorities. To equate smoking with alcohol or drugs as teenage dangers is obviously absurd, and would never have happened if the health dangers of smoking had been accurately reported. The war on smoking has become a crusade of good against evil, and logic and science have been prostituted to attain its objective.

THE SOUL-CORRUPTING ANTITOBACCO CRUSADE

Dennis Prager

America's war against tobacco and teen smoking is morally irresponsible, maintains Dennis Prager in the following piece. Policymakers exaggerate the bad effects of cigarette smoking while downplaying the more serious dangers of drug use, alcohol abuse, and unwed motherhood, Prager writes. Moreover, he points out, antitobacco crusaders who claim that cigarette advertising causes people to smoke give teens the destructive message that they are not personally responsible for their actions. Prager is an author, theologian, and radio talk-show host based in Los Angeles, California.

I have never been a cigarette smoker. I have never doubted that cigarette smoking is dangerous. I believe that American tobacco companies have systematically lied about the dangers of cigarettes. I accept the public-health statistic that one out of three cigarette smokers will die prematurely.

I have smoked a pipe and cigars since I was a teenager. The joy and relaxation that cigars and pipes have brought me are very great. I do not regret having begun smoking. Life does not afford us an unlimited number of daily pleasures that are as largely innocuous as cigar and pipe smoking. As for my three children, I would not be particularly concerned if they decided to smoke cigars or pipes, and while I would be unhappy if they took up cigarette smoking and became addicted to nicotine, I would not be unduly so. I would be considerably more unhappy if they became addicted to television. In fact, if smoking cigarettes is the most dangerous activity or worst vice my children ever engage in, I will rejoice.

I therefore do not consider cigarette smoking, let alone cigar or pipe smoking, to be worthy of the crusade society is waging against it. A simple common-sense health problem has been transformed into America's great moral cause. In the process, the war against smoking is playing havoc with moral values—with the truth, with science and scientists, with children's moral education, with the war on real drugs, with the principle of personal freedom and much more that we hold dear. The war against tobacco, in short, has come to be far more dangerous than tobacco itself.

Equating Tobacco Use with Drug Use

One particularly irresponsible aspect of the war against tobacco is the now commonplace equating of tobacco use with drug use. In California, which leads the country in sums spent on anti-smoking ads, billboards throughout the state proclaim that cigarettes and tobacco are drugs—implicitly no different from marijuana or even heroin and cocaine. In fact, it has become a staple of anti-smoking rhetoric that it is harder to end nicotine addiction than heroin addiction. Now the anti-smoking forces want the Food and Drug Administration to regulate nicotine as a drug.

The only conceivable consequence of equating hard drugs, which can destroy the mind and soul, with tobacco, which can actually have positive effects on the mind and has no deleterious effect on the soul, is to lessen the fear of real drugs among young people. How could it not? If taking heroin, cocaine, and marijuana is the moral, personal, and social equivalent of smoking cigarettes, then how bad can heroin, cocaine, and marijuana be? After all, young people see adults smoking cigarettes all the time without destroying their lives.

The truth is that tobacco doesn't interfere with the soul, mind, conscience, or emotional growth of a smoker. As for the one trait cigarettes and drugs share—addictiveness—this tells us little. Human beings are addicted to a plethora of substances and activities. These include coffee, sugar, alcohol, gambling, sex, food, spending, and virtually every other human endeavor that brings immediate gratification and that people cannot, or choose not to, control.

In the past, when the moral compass of our society functioned more accurately, we fought the addictions that lead to social breakdown far more vigorously than those that can lead to ill health. Today American society and government do the opposite: They fight health dangers—and actually encourage social dangers. For example, government now encourages gambling (by instituting lotteries and legalizing casinos, which advertise more freely than tobacco); government largely ignores alcohol, the addiction most associated with child abuse, spousal abuse, and violent crime; and it fails in its efforts to curb real drug addiction. All the while, it wages its most ubiquitous war against cigarette smokers, who pose no danger to society or family life.

The Demonization of Smokers

Another irresponsible aspect of the war against tobacco is the demonization of smokers. In the span of a few years, smokers have been transformed from people engaged in a somewhat dangerous but morally innocuous habit into drug addicts, child abusers, and killers.

Smoking has become, incredibly, an issue of moral character, not merely of health.

Here is one result:

> Judges in divorce cases are increasingly considering smoking as a factor in deciding where to put the kids and retaining custody. . . . If a judge is so inclined, he can depict smoking as negative in two ways: dirtying the child's air and *showing poor character.*

> In Knox County, Tenn., the Circuit Court has adopted a rule for all custody cases, and *not just those in which the child has a health problem:* "If children are exposed to smoke, it will be strong evidence that the exposing parent does not take good care of them."

> That rule led last year to a criminal contempt conviction— and a loss of all visitation rights—for a father who smoked during his time with his daughter. [Associated Press, April 18, 1997, italics added.]

Think of it: A thoroughly decent person and loving parent can now lose custody of his or her child solely because of smoking. This is moral idiocy, and it hinges on the fraudulent theory of secondhand smoke.

Since the Environmental Protection Agency listed secondhand smoke as a first-class human carcinogen in 1993, numerous eminent scientists have expressed skepticism. They include epidemiologists Dimitrios Trichopoulos of the Harvard School of Public Health and Alvan Feinstein of Yale Medical School. Dr. Philippe Shubik, editor in chief of *Teratogenesis, Carcinogenesis and Mutagenesis,* published at Oxford University, contrasts cigarette smoking—"an unequivocal human cancer hazard"—with environmental smoke. Officially designating the latter a human carcinogen, he writes, "is not only unjustified but establishes a scientifically unsound principle."

In other words, anti-tobacco activists who ascribe murderous carcinogenic qualities to secondhand smoke are engaging in junk science and propaganda, just as were the pro-tobacco spokesmen who denied the carcinogenic properties of smoking.

Brainwashing Children

Instilling fear in children has been one of the few successful educational techniques in America over the past generation. Educators frightened young children first about dying in a nuclear war; then about dying from heterosexually transmitted AIDS; then about being sexually harassed; then about being abused (hence teachers and day-care providers are told not to hug children); then about "stranger danger"; and now schools tell our children that their parent who smokes will die and may even kill them.

After frightening young children, the anti-smoking crusaders attempt to use them: Children's grasp of the issue is not terribly sophisticated, which makes them all the more easily brainwashed and all the more useful as foot soldiers in the war against smoking.

Massachusetts—a state that prides itself on its commitment to "question authority"—puts its students to work unquestioningly on behalf of anti-smoking authority. Thus, second-graders in Mattapan are told to express their support for a smoking ban in restaurants. Fifth-graders in Chelsea are instructed to use an approach reminiscent of the Chinese Cultural Revolution, namely, "to knock on the doors of friends and parents who smoke to educate them about the dangers of smoking."

But frightening children is hardly the only abuse of which the anti-smoking zealots are guilty. Lies, half-truths, exaggerations, and distortions characterize the anti-smoking campaign—as much as they ever characterized the tobacco companies.

Manipulating the Truth

The first manipulation of truth concerns the number of Americans said to die from smoking. We are told repeatedly that 500,000 Americans die each year from "tobacco-related illnesses." Even if the figure is accurate, citing it as if it were the only relevant statistic is dishonest.

What if anti-smoking billboards and ads told the truth about the two statistics that truly matter to anyone contemplating smoking: What are the chances that any individual smoker will die prematurely? And how many years does the average pack-a-day cigarette smoker lose? If anti-smoking announcements dealt with these questions, they would have to declare something like this: "One out of every three cigarette smokers will die prematurely," and, "While the average American male who never smoked a cigarette will live until age 78, males who smoke a pack a day will, on average, live only until age 71."

That's it. The justification for all this hysteria—all the laws restricting speech in advertisements, all the bans on smoking sections in private businesses, all the regressive taxes, all this frightening of children about their lives and those of their parents—is that one-third of cigarette smokers die prematurely, at an average loss of seven years. And that may overstate the case. According to *The Costs of Poor Health Habits*, a RAND study published in 1991 by Harvard University Press, smoking cigarettes "reduces the life expectancy of a 20-year-old by about 4.3 years."

Another claim, repeated by President Clinton in a radio broadcast in June 1998, is that we must fight tobacco in order to "save the lives of one million young people." I will leave it to others to determine whether this qualifies as a lie or sophistry. Whichever, it is untrue.

Unlike drugs, drunk driving, and murder, which annually kill many thousands of young people, cigarettes do not kill a single young person. Those young people who die from cigarettes will do so at an average age of over 70. Tell that to the young.

One of the greatest distortions of truth by the anti-smoking crusade—one that can only be characterized as a Big Lie, since it is repeated so often, by so many, and has led to a money grab of unprecedented proportions—is how much it costs the public to cover the medical care of smokers.

We are told that treatment of sick smokers costs government billions of dollars a year. Unlike the claim of 500,000 a year dead from "tobacco-related diseases," which is only misleading and can be neither proved nor disproved, this claim is easily exposed as a lie. Smokers actually save the public money. On purely financial grounds, the public is a net gainer from cigarette smokers. To put it differently: If everyone stopped smoking, the public would lose substantial sums.

This is because government makes a great deal of money from cigarette taxes, and it saves enormous sums upon the death of cigarette smokers, most of whom die at an age when they would otherwise collect Social Security and other public benefits. Moreover, as hard as it is for the anti-smoking movement to acknowledge, non-smokers impose great costs on society in their last months of life, just as smokers do.

Misplaced Priorities

Society has always had two means of discouraging behavior: punishment and stigma. What a society punishes and stigmatizes reveals what it values.

Consider a recent cover story in *People* magazine. The cover featured a photograph of actress Jody Foster, who was pregnant. The magazine overflowed with enthusiasm about her pregnancy and quoted one source after another welcoming the future Foster child.

This article would have been inconceivable a generation ago. For not only is Jody Foster unmarried, there is not even an identifiable father (presumably some anonymous sperm donor) for the child she is bringing into the world.

Yet this means nothing to elite America. Hooray for the deliberately fatherless child! Hooray for unwed motherhood! Those are the messages sent to America's young women and girls and to its young men and boys.

People magazine, a pretty accurate reflection of America's social attitudes, knew it ran no risk by celebrating a fatherless pregnancy. But there is one photo it would probably never dare show on its cover: Jody Foster smoking a cigarette.

America has made its choice: It reserves its stigma for cigarette smokers and is entirely nonjudgmental about bringing children into the world without a father. When I see smokers shivering outside buildings and regarded by many as pathetic or even dangerous people while unwed mothers are celebrated, I worry about America's future.

Here's another example of the misplaced priorities that the hysteria over cigarette smoking has wrought. The president of the United States and the country's surgeon general summoned the national media to the White House for what they deemed a highly significant announcement: Smoking among black and other minority youths has increased. President Bill Clinton and Surgeon General David Satcher appeared with a group of non-white children and spoke in the gravest tones about this threat to them.

But in his years in office, the president has never convened a White House conference to lament the plague of unwed motherhood. The majority of black children grow up without their father in their home. This is easily the greatest obstacle to black progress. Yet the president and the media focus on the increase in cigarette smoking among young blacks—and black smoking rates are *lower* than those of whites.

A question: Which would improve black life more—for every single black youth to stop smoking while the illegitimacy rate remained the same, or for every black youth to smoke cigarettes while growing up from birth to adulthood with both of his parents? With the nation morally at sea, many Americans may find this question difficult to answer.

Denying Personal Responsibility

At the heart of the anti-smoking lawsuits against the tobacco industry is the denial that smokers are personally responsible for smoking. They allegedly had no knowledge of the dangers of cigarette smoking and began smoking because venal tobacco companies used mind-numbing ads to convince them cigarettes were healthy.

The last thing America needs is a massive campaign further eroding personal responsibility. We already live in a country that regularly teaches its citizens to blame others—government, ads, parents, schools, movies, genes, sugar, tobacco, alcohol, sexism, racism—for their poor decisions and problems. Now we have the largest public-relations campaign in American history teaching Americans this: If you smoke, you are in no way responsible for what happens to you. You are entirely a victim.

The war against tobacco is telling teenagers in particular to look for others to blame. The latest ad campaign, in Florida—funded by tens of millions of public dollars—is directed to teens. It tells them that if they smoke, they do so solely because they have been manipulated by tobacco-company ads. This is the theme of all the approaches to young people by the anti-smoking forces: You kids have been manipulated by a cartoon camel.

This approach not only sends the destructive message to young people that they are not responsible for their behavior, that they are helpless when confronted with a billboard for Marlboro cigarettes, it also is intellectually dishonest. If young people are powerless in the face of tobacco billboards—tobacco ads are already banned from television, radio, and youth-oriented magazines—they are presumably powerless in the face of all advertisements. Why then allow advertisements for liquor, wine, beer, or R-rated movies? Aren't young people equally powerless in the face of these ads? Why allow ads showing sexually suggestive gestures or behavior? Won't those ads make young people engage in sex? Or is teen sex less worrisome than teen smoking? Isn't the message that young people are not responsible for behaving as billboards urge them to behave a *disempowering* message?

Why Is America Obsessed with Smoking?

The ultimate question is this: Why, given the far greater ills of American society and the minimal harm caused by tobacco, is America obsessed with smoking? The reason is that our moral compass is broken. Two generations ago, when our value system was comparatively sound, the vice America fought was alcohol, not tobacco. America understood that the effects of alcohol are incomparably worse than the effects of tobacco.

Cigarettes can lead to premature death. Alcohol can lead to murder, rape, child abuse, spousal beatings, family rupture, and permanent pathologies in the children of alcoholics. If all alcoholic beverages were miraculously removed from the earth, the amount of rape, murder, child abuse, and spousal beating would plummet, and no child would ever again suffer the permanently debilitating effects of having been raised by an alcoholic. If all tobacco products miraculously disappeared from the earth, the amount of rape, murder, child abuse, and spousal beating would remain identical, and millions of children would continue to suffer the horrors of growing up in alcoholic homes. In other words, morally speaking, little would change if tobacco miraculously disappeared.

In a more religious age, social activists fought alcohol; in our secular age, social activists fight tobacco—and a few other select ills, such as restrictions on abortion. Indeed, America's elites now consider it immoral to let a bar owner choose whether to allow smoking in his bar. But the same elites are pro-choice when it comes to letting the alcohol flow in those bars and allowing mothers to extinguish nascent human life for any reason they please.

The same president who vetoed a bill outlawing "partial-birth" abortions, which are usually performed in mid or late pregnancy, vigorously opposes choice about smoking in nearly all privately owned businesses. In California at the end of the twentieth century, third-trimester abortions are legal, but smoking in bars and outdoor stadiums is not. I happen to favor keeping first-trimester abortions legal, but even I can see that it is quite a statement about a society's sense of right and wrong when it deems secondhand smoke more worthy of legal restriction than the killing of human fetuses.

The Dangers of the Anti-Smoking Crusade

As early as 1994, *New York Times* columnist Russell Baker foresaw the dangers of the anti-smoking crusade. He wrote:

> Crusades typically start by being admirable, proceed to being foolish and end by being dangerous. The crusade against smoking is now clearly well into the second stage where foolishness abounds.
>
> Now something very sinister is developing. Some businesses are refusing to hire workers who smoke outside the workplace, on the grounds that smokers' health problems are bad for their employers.
>
> This is an illustration of a crusade entering its dangerous stage. Give employers the right to control the habits of their workers outside the workplace, and you set the stage for a tyranny even worse than the evils of too much government which keep conservatives so alarmed.

Put this crusade in perspective. In the 1920s, America waged a war against alcohol. In the 1930s, it battled economic depression. In the 1940s, it fought fascism. In the 1950s and 1960s, it led the struggle against communism. In the 1970s, America grappled with its own racism and bigotry. In the 1980s, it ensured the defeat of the Soviet empire.

The next generation will ask: What preoccupied America in the final decade of the twentieth century—while unprecedented numbers of its children were being raised without fathers, while the country was living with rates of murder far higher than in any other advanced democracy, while its public schools were graduating semi-literates, while its ability to fight two wars was being eviscerated even as rogue nations built stocks of chemical and biological weapons and new countries were acquiring nuclear weapons? The editors of America's leading editorial pages and the majority of its national politicians, state attorneys general, and educators will be able to answer together, "We fought tobacco." Shame on them all.

THE MISUSE OF CHILDREN IN ANTITOBACCO PROPAGANDA

Jacob Sullum

In the following selection, Jacob Sullum contends that tobacco opponents often use young people in propagandistic news releases and public service announcements to fuel antismoking fervor. Using intentionally skewed statistics about the number of teenagers who smoke cigarettes, antitobacco crusaders mislead the public about the prevalence and effects of underage smoking, argues Sullum. Moreover, he maintains, the ultimate goal of the antitobacco policymakers is to ban smoking altogether—not simply to curb teen smoking. Sullum is a senior editor of *Reason*, a monthly libertarian journal. He is also the author of *For Your Own Good: The Anti-Smoking Crusade and the Tyranny of Public Health*.

"Every Day, Without Action on Tobacco, 1,000 Kids Will Die Early." So says the headline of an ad on the op-ed page of the *New York Times*, conjuring up images of fifth-graders dying from lung cancer, 12-year-olds keeling over with heart attacks in the cafeteria, and high-school sophomores with emphysema wheezing as they climb the stairs on the way to their next class. The ad, sponsored by the National Center for Tobacco-Free Kids, is aimed at obscuring the fact that smokers die from their habit only after they've been puffing away for decades—putting them well into adulthood, by most people's standards.

Such propaganda is part of a broader effort to pretend that the antismoking crusade is about protecting "kids" from the Merchants of Death, when in reality it is about protecting adults from themselves. Saving the children has been offered as a rationale for higher cigarette taxes, restrictions on advertising and promotion, lawsuits against the tobacco companies, regulation of cigarettes by the Food and Drug Administration, and just about every other policy aimed at discouraging smoking. It is sure to be a persistent theme as Congress continues to debate tobacco legislation. White House advisor Rahm Emanuel describes the choice confronting legislators this way: "They can either stand shoulder to shoulder with corporate tobacco and their profits or protect our children and ensure their health and safety."

Misinformation

To get a sense of how misleading this is, consider a few numbers. In the 1996 National Household Survey on Drug Abuse, 29 per cent of the respondents had smoked cigarettes during the previous month (not necessarily every day). That translates into about 62 million Americans aged 12 and older. Of them, 4 million, or about 6 per cent, were under 18. In other words, more than 90 per cent of the smokers who would be affected by the anti-tobacco measures Congress is now considering—including proposals that would nearly double the price of cigarettes—are adults.

OK, say tobacco's opponents, the vast majority of smokers are adults. But they weren't always. "We know that three thousand children start smoking every day," President Clinton said in 1996, responding to Philip Morris's signal that it was prepared to accept restrictions on advertising and promotion. "We are concerned about the three thousand kids who become addicted every day," said Matthew Myers of the National Center for Tobacco-Free Kids.

That estimate, which has been endlessly repeated by activists, public officials, and the press, comes from an article published in the *Journal of the American Medical Association* (*JAMA*) in January 1989. Based on data from the National Health Interview Survey, the authors estimated that 1 million "young persons" became regular smokers each year in the early 1980s, which amounts to about three thousand a day. This figure refers to 20-year-olds, since the study did not include data for anyone younger than that. Somehow these "young persons" metamorphosed into Myers's "kids" and Clinton's "children." At least one commentator (on CNBC) referred to them as "babies."

Now, it's true that most smokers—more than 70 per cent, according to the 1994 Surgeon General's report—are not legally adults when they start lighting up regularly. But they are not exactly "children" either: According to the National Household Survey on Drug Abuse, the mean age of people who started smoking daily in 1995 was 17.6. Yet the National Center for Tobacco-Free Kids runs ads that consistently portray smokers who look to be 11 or 12. According to the Monitoring the Future Study, which is overseen by the National Institute on Drug Abuse, fewer than 1 in 10 eighth-graders smokes so much as a cigarette a day.

Are Smokers Enslaved by Nicotine?

I am focusing on daily smoking—instead of, say, the first cigarette—because occasional smokers cannot reasonably be described as addicts, and tobacco's opponents claim that smokers are enslaved by nicotine before they're old enough to know better. As former Food and Drug Administration Commissioner David A. Kessler once put it, "Nicotine addiction is a pediatric disease that often begins at 12, 13, and 14, only to manifest itself at 16 and 17, when these children find they cannot quit. By then our children have lost their freedom and face the prospect of lives shortened by terrible disease."

This is the standard response to anyone who asks, "So what if people start smoking as teenagers? After they become adults, they've got plenty of time to quit before any lasting damage is done." Not so, says Kessler. Once they start, smokers cannot quit. They "have lost their freedom."

The problem with this argument is that it flies in the face of every-day experience. People quit smoking all the time. The same study that generated the three-thousand-children-a-day factoid estimated that between 1974 and 1985, about 1.3 million Americans quit smoking each year. According to the U.S. Centers for Disease Control and Prevention, there are about as many former smokers in this country as there are smokers, and 90 per cent of them stopped without formal treatment, typically by quitting cold turkey. As then-Surgeon General C. Everett Koop noted in his 1984 speech calling for "a smoke-free society," smoking "is a voluntary act: one does not have to smoke if one does not want to."

But since quitting is often difficult, many Americans are understandably concerned about the recent rise in smoking by teenagers. Underage smoking declined more or less steadily from the late 1970s until 1992, then rose for several years in a row. In the Monitoring the Future Study, the percentage of high-school seniors who were daily smokers rose from 17.2 in 1992 to 21.6 in 1995. That was still well below the 1977 peak of 28.8, and the trend now seems to have leveled off. During the same period, marijuana use by teenagers also rose, following a 13-year decline. Yet this group of teenagers had been bombarded by the most intense antitobacco and anti-pot propaganda in U.S. history. By telling these kids, "Just Say No," the schools, the media, and the government may have taught them a more appealing lesson: how to offend adults.

Creating a Smoke-Free Society?

In addition to the potential for backlash among rebellious adolescents, tobacco opponents should recognize that their efforts to reduce underage smoking might not have much of an impact on smoking by adults. Anti-smokers tend to assume that if everyone could be shielded from cigarettes until the age of 18 (or 21), virtually no one would smoke. As a recent *JAMA* article about tobacco advertising put it, "Once people are old enough to rationally evaluate the well-known health risks of smoking, they choose not to start." In *Smokescreen*, journalist Philip Hilts flatly asserts: "Adults do not start smoking."

But this is not the case even now: a minority of smokers do start as adults, and that group is likely to expand if efforts to discourage underage smoking are successful. While it may be true that the young are especially attracted to smoking, it is probably also true that people who are especially attracted to smoking tend to start young. Each individual's tastes, personality, and circumstances will determine whether keeping him away from cigarettes until he is an adult will prevent smoking or simply delay it.

Some anti-smokers have publicly complained about the focus on teenagers. "The anti-tobacco movement has careened off on this narrow path because they know it's noncontroversial," longtime anti-smoking activist Stanton Glantz told the *New York Times* in 1996. "But it's probably counterproductive. A kid-centered program is doomed to fail." Glantz worries that depicting smoking as an adult habit makes it more appealing to kids and lets the vast majority of smokers off the hook. "The best way to keep kids from smoking is to reduce tobacco consumption among everyone," he writes in the *American Journal of Public Health.* "The message should not be, 'We don't want kids to smoke'; it should be, 'We want a smoke-free society.'"

At a June 1997 meeting of the Advisory Committee on Tobacco Policy and Public Health, a panel chaired by Drs. Koop and Kessler, participants reminded their colleagues that they should not be blinded by their own save-the-children rhetoric. "The goal is not just to reduce childhood addiction to nicotine and to tobacco products," said Mark Pertschuk of Americans for Nonsmokers' Rights. "It's also to reduce adult addiction to levels which are feasible." Michele Bloch of the American Medical Women's Association made the same point: "I would ask that in our own recommendations, in addition to putting youth as our top priority, we not tie our hands from working on reducing adult smoking through penalties, etc., when the time comes." Stock up while you can.

CHAPTER 2

WHY DO TEENAGERS SMOKE CIGARETTES?

THE SMOKING GUN: PROOF THAT TOBACCO COMPANIES MARKETED TO TEENS

Barry Meier

Tobacco company records released to the public in January 1998 prove that cigarette manufacturers intentionally marketed their product to teenagers, Barry Meier reports. R.J. Reynolds documents, for example, reveal that the company planned to heavily advertise in areas frequented by youths and to increase sales of its products among smokers as young as fourteen. Although tobacco industry spokespersons deny that they intended to sell cigarettes to those under eighteen, Meier writes, the released evidence indicates that cigarette companies compete for underage customers because teenage smokers are more likely to switch brands than adults are. Meier is a reporter for the *New York Times*.

Internal records from one of the nation's largest cigarette companies, R.J. Reynolds Tobacco, provide new evidence of the extent to which the company for decades courted young smokers, including some as young as 14, regarding them as the future of its business.

As recently as 1988, for example, R.J. Reynolds planned to saturate areas where young people gathered, like fast-food restaurants, video game arcades and outdoor basketball courts, with billboards and posters promoting its products, one memorandum shows. Other documents among the papers released to the public on January 14, 1998, emphasized that the company sought to expand sales of its products among underage smokers, including those age 14, in order to sustain brand popularity and corporate earnings.

"To ensure increased and longer-term growth for Camel filter," one internal 1975 company memorandum stated, "the brand must increase its share penetration among the 14–24 age group, which have a new set of more liberal values and which represent tomorrow's cigarette business."

These are not the first documents to suggest that Reynolds and other tobacco companies sought to court youthful smokers. But the documents made public in January 1998 are among the most explicit to have been released. And, while company officials have attributed previous documents on youth marketing to low-level or renegade employees, some of these documents show the involvement of top company officials, including directors, in the 1970's.

Officials of R.J. Reynolds, a unit of the RJR Nabisco Holdings Corporation, have repeatedly denied in public statements and sworn testimony that they sought to sell cigarettes to those under 18. And on January 14, 1998, Peggy Carter, a company spokeswoman, restated that position, saying that the documents at issue had been selectively released by plaintiffs' lawyers to appear out of context. [In the mid-1990s, several individuals and groups sued the tobacco industry, claiming that their health had been harmed by smoking.]

Ms. Carter said R.J. Reynolds officials did not have time to fully address specific documents. But the company said in a statement: "Our documents reflect the social attitudes of the times in which they were created. And while attitudes toward smoking have changed over the past several decades, the Reynolds Tobacco Company's position and policy has remained constant: that smoking is a choice for adults and that marketing programs are directed at those above the age to smoke."

Dr. David A. Kessler, the former Commissioner of Food and Drugs who began that agency's inquiry into the tobacco advertising practices, said the newly released documents were the strongest evidence yet of a major company's effort to focus on youth.

"These are as close to smoking guns when it comes to targeting kids" as have ever appeared, said Dr. Kessler, who is dean of Yale University Medical School.

Advertising Appeal

Viewed together, the R.J. Reynolds documents indicate that top tobacco industry executives long believed that people under 18 were its most crucial customers because by that age, minors who smoked had chosen the brand that they would stick with and smoke even more as adults. While the documents do not show that the company directly advocated persuading children to start smoking, they do strongly suggest that R.J. Reynolds wanted its share of those children who did smoke.

For example, a marketing plan prepared in late 1974 for the board of directors of R.J. Reynolds noted that company brands like Winston, Salem, and Camel were increasingly losing ground among 14- to 24-year old smokers to Marlboro brand cigarettes made by the Philip Morris Companies.

"This suggests slow market share erosion for us in years to come unless the situation is corrected," the document stated. One company strategy to combat that trend would be to "direct advertising appeal" to those younger smokers, the plan said.

Among the techniques suggested in the plan were advertisements in magazines read by young people, like *Sports Illustrated, Playboy* and *Ms.*, and the sponsorship of sports events like auto racing.

At the time the marketing plan was presented to the company's top executives, it was illegal in most states to sell cigarettes to those under 18.

Fears Were Justified

Representative Henry Waxman, Democrat of California and a long-time tobacco industry opponent, said that he believed that the company documents clashed with Congressional testimony by R.J. Reynolds executives. For example, he pointed to a 1994 statement by James W. Johnston, then the company's chief executive, that R.J. Reynolds did "not market to children and will not."

"I think these documents show that our worst fears about the tobacco companies going after our kids were justified," said Mr. Waxman, who said he planned to refer the R.J. Reynolds documents to the Justice Department which is investigating possible fraud by tobacco producers.

Ms. Carter, the R.J. Reynolds spokeswoman, disputed any contentions that Mr. Johnston or any other company official had not been forthcoming in their testimony or public statements.

The release of the documents came as Congress is set to consider a $368.5 billion settlement proposal reached in June 1997 between tobacco producers, including R.J. Reynolds, and state attorneys general. Under one portion of that plan, cigarette producers would pay fines if youth smoking failed to fall in the future, but Mr. Waxman and other critics of the proposal have said the fines in it should be strengthened and meted out company by company, rather than industrywide. [This settlement was revised and finalized in November 1998.]

The Death of Joe Camel

R.J. Reynolds first handed over the documents during a lawsuit filed in 1991 against the company's "Joe Camel" advertising campaign by Janet Mangini, a lawyer in San Francisco, and several California cities and counties. The lawsuit was settled in September 1997, and R.J. Reynolds agreed to the public release of the documents as part of the settlement. In 1997, R.J. Reynolds dropped its Joe Camel campaign after criticism by antismoking advocates and government regulators that the cartoon-like figure was attracting underage smokers to the brand.

The documents made available in January 1998 show that for decades, the company commissioned or subscribed to surveys that tracked the smoking habits of teen-agers, including those as young as 14. While some R.J. Reynolds memorandums stated that the surveys were not to be used for marketing, the data produced in the studies were reviewed by the company's highest officers, a company memorandum indicates.

In 1980, for example, Gerald H. Long, the company's top marketing executive at the time, wrote to Edward A. Horrigan, then chief executive of R.J. Reynolds, to warn him that the company's flagship Winston brand was increasingly losing sales among "14–17 year old smokers" to Marlboro cigarettes.

"Hopefully, our various planned activities that will be implemented this fall will aid in some way in reducing and correcting these trends," wrote Mr. Long, who subsequently became chief executive of R.J. Reynolds.

In responding to the document released in 1997, David W. Donahue, R.J. Reynolds's deputy counsel, had said in a statement that Mr. Long had subsequently expressed concern that someone would surmise from the memorandum that the company planned to market cigarettes to children.

"He was adamant that the company firmly adhered to its position that youth should not smoke and that it would direct its marketing efforts only at adult smokers," Mr. Donahue said in 1997. "The record across the board supports that."

The Significance of Underage Smokers

Two years after Mr. Long's memorandum was written, Mr. Horrigan testified before Congress that charges that industry advertising and promotional practices were intended to promote youth smoking were "without foundation."

After 1980, the R.J. Reynolds documents do not discuss children, referring instead to those ages 18 to 24 as "younger adult smokers." But company studies and documents emphasized the critical importance of underage smokers to the future of cigarette makers like R.J. Reynolds.

In a 1984 internal R.J. Reynolds report "Younger Adult Smokers: Strategies and Opportunities," a top company researcher, Diane S. Burrows, wrote that the "renewal of the market stems almost entirely from 18-year-old smokers" because fewer than 5 percent of smokers started after age 24 and the company's ability to get them to switch brands far outweighed their brand loyalty.

A few years later, R.J. Reynolds started its controversial advertising campaign using Joe Camel. Tobacco industry officials have consistently asserted that peer pressure, rather than advertising, leads young people to start smoking. But a 1986 company memorandum that discussed ways to attract 18 to 24 year olds recommended that a new Camel advertising campaign be directed toward "using peer acceptance/ influence to provide the motivation for target smokers to select Camel."

Marketing plans for the Joe Camel campaign called for saturating outdoor areas with billboards and posters, a company memorandum shows. While some advertisements in some selected areas, like college campuses, would reach those over 18, other locations, like fast-food restaurants and video game arcades, are frequented by minors.

Youths Are Bombarded by Cigarette Ads

Gene Borio

In the supermarkets, on billboards, and in magazines, young people are inundated daily with advertisements for cigarettes, reports Gene Borio. Tobacco products are also prominently featured in movies and on television shows, he writes. The pervasiveness of such tobacco marketing makes smoking seem acceptable and innocuous and has led to an increase in teen smoking, the author contends. Borio is a freelance writer and a computer and telecommunications specialist living in Village Station, New York. He has been active in antitobacco efforts since the 1980s.

7:00 AM: There goes his radio alarm, with his favorite station blaring promotions for Virginia Slims Tennis or Marlboro Racing.

At breakfast, his mother sets out the cereal box—you know, the "Kellogg's Corn Flakes Winston Cup Commemorative" edition, with cigarette brand name "Winston" splashed on every side, and nary a health warning in sight. When his own mom advertises cigarettes to him with his corn flakes, he's got to wonder—geez, how bad can they be?

At the bus shelter, he sits under the Marlboro Man poster. On the bus, he rides past billboard after billboard hawking cigarettes. There are warnings on the billboards—can you see? It's that little white band at the bottom, printed in an unreadable font and style. The industry's policy is that they want no billboards within 500 feet of a school. That's the distance at which the warning becomes completely illegible.

Growing Up with Cigarette Ads

Once at school, a friend shows off his Kool baseball cap, and the neat lighter he just got for "Camel Cash." Another got ahold of a "Newport Pleasure" t-shirt. One kid even has a Marlboro Panasonic disc player! Yeah, you're supposed to be 21 to get them (giggle-giggle).

After school, a stop by the convenience store—you can't even see inside the store, there are so many tobacco posters littering the windows. Once inside, it's a veritable deluge of promotional materials, with the cigarettes right out front for the picking (or shoplifting). Of

Reprinted, with permission, from "An Ad-erage Day in the Life of a Kid," by Gene Borio, a 1996 Web article published at www.tobacco.org/Misc/kids_ad_day.html.

course, they're nothing new—they've always been there, ever since he was old enough to stretch up to the ad-filled counter to buy a candy bar. You might say he's grown up with them.

And it's not just this store—everywhere he goes, from the tiniest country town that only has one store, to the biggest city, the ads are everywhere. Their very ubiquity is an argument for smoking, and that argument goes—hey! no big deal. They're everywhere. Why fight it? Who cares? Not these store owners.

He buys a *Rolling Stone* magazine, where all the glittering promotional prizes are presented in luscious color, to be had for a few cigarette pack coupons, and the little white lie of averring he's 21. (He knows they don't check too hard.)

Colorful cigarette ads fill his favorite magazines like jewelry, slick and enticing. No wonder he associates music, sports and youth culture with cigarettes—they fit so neatly, so coolly into the whole ambiance presented by *Rolling Stone* and other entertainment magazines. And not a single article dares to offer the slightest counterpoint to that message, repeated page after page, magazine after magazine, month after month, year after year. . . .

Cigarette Promotion Is Everywhere

At home, he catches a little baseball, and watches a thrilling home run go right over the Marlboro sign. Seems that Marlboro sign is situated where almost every home run is near it. In other sports, the sign always seems to be right by the clock. In auto racing, the really tough trick is to find the shots in which a cigarette brand is not shown.

Then it's time for his dad to take him to the doctor's for a checkup. On the way they stop for gas, and he's sent inside to pay—he almost has to snake his hand past all the cigarette promotionals on the counter to give the clerk the money. He's got to figure if Mobil and Esso don't have a problem with cigarettes, what's the big deal?

In the doctor's waiting room, the mainstream magazines like *Time* or *Vanity Fair* feature more cigarette ads on their back covers. At his sister's asthma clinic, it's not unusual to see a pre-schooler's book on the table, right next to a big flashy Joe Camel ad on the back of an adult's magazine. And those Joe Camel ads are just as worthy of curious study as anything out of *Where the Wild Things Are*. In fact, the kid's book looks pretty dull next to Joe's pizazz. How bad could cigarettes be if even doctors are advertising them? [In 1997, ads featuring the cartoon character Joe Camel were discontinued.]

They stop to fill the prescription. At McKay's Drug Stores, Love's Pharmacies, CVS, or Duane Reade in New York City, they have a Pharmacist in back and a Harm-assist in front—Joe Camel himself feigning cool in a huge display over the cashier line. And in many stores, tobacco has moved out to the shelves—look at all the chewing tobacco and cigars in the aisle right opposite the Pharmacist. These are the people who are supposed to be knowledgeable about your health. If tobacco is being so heavily promoted even here—hey, really, how bad could they be?

On the way back home, they stop for a few things at the supermarket—Grand Union, or Sloan's here in New York City. Dad unconsciously picks up a Marlboro hand-basket. Hey, if even Dad can act as a walking human billboard for them, how bad can they be?

Cigarettes in Movies and on TV

Home to watch TV. Let's see, what's on, where's that TV Guide. Ah, here we are, right past the "Misty" ad—*Superman II* at 8 PM. That's the one where Superman crashes spectacularly into the side of a Marlboro-emblazoned truck. Or maybe he'll watch tough-guy Sylvester Stallone in a movie hawking Brown & Williamson cigarettes, just as Sly agreed to do for $500,000. Or that 1997 blockbuster, *Independence Day,* the most spectacular and expensive cigar commercial ever filmed. Will Smith *stops saving the world* until he can get a couple of cigars. "This is important!" he says. And indeed, by the end of the film, even anti-cigar fuddy-duddy (and *Cigar Aficionado* cover boy) Jeff Goldblum is cool now, and enjoys a victory cigar with Smith (product placement by Feature This).

Or maybe he'll watch some car racing like the Grand Prix, where Al Unser Jr. whizzes his "Marlboro" car by the cameras a documented 39,000 times in each race. You're 9 years old and you like car racing? Then you'd better like cigarettes, 'cause Al Unser Jr. doesn't drive the Sunkist Orange Juice car.

Or how about just a plain TV show, like *Seinfeld*—the one where Kramer hands out "Big Butt" cigars to Jerry and George (product placement by A-List Placements).

But now it's time for his favorite movie review program, *Siskel and Ebert*—the single most smoking-packed program on TV, with more shots of people—major movie stars, unknowns, young, old and in between, all sorts of glamorous people—smoking coolly per minute than any other regular show. There's hardly a movie, of course, that addresses the consequences of smoking, so these are never seen, or even referred to. The message is loud and clear.

His friend is sixteen, and can use his folks' car, so they're going to go out this weekend. He picked up one of those freebie city papers—the *Village Voice* or the *New York Press*, here in New York—and of course they are positively festooned with cigarette ads. Nightlife, music, movies—everything seems to go naturally with cigarettes. And no one says a word against it. What's a kid to think?

He's up a little late, but maybe he'll catch that cool David Letterman. In the introductory montage, there's Joe Camel winking at him from a 42nd St. billboard. And during Letterman's monologue, you can clearly see that the red-and-black patch in the background is a classic

Marlboro ad. (In countries with strong cigarette advertising restrictions, marketers have succeeded in associating their product with more abstract qualities—all "Silk Cut" has to do, for example, is show a swath of purple silk and the "branding" for that cigarette is complete.)

There is no wonder why kid smoking is skyrocketing. Admittedly, I've condensed a lot into one day, but this is more than made up for by the fact that I listed each incident only once, whereas most occur over and over and over again, day after day after day, ad nauseam.

A Relentless Onslaught

Kids today are faced with a relentless, daily, almost hourly, mind-numbing, spirit-debilitating, reality-bending onslaught of tobacco ads, and the presentation of tobacco use as a nearly universal and cool activity. Not hard to see why more 6-year-olds recognize Joe Camel than Mickey Mouse.

And never, ever underestimate the power of ubiquity. The ads are everywhere, all the time—and ubiquity buys acceptance. Why go against the stream? Why make trouble by objecting? Everyone else seems to accept it.

And who's this "everyone else"? Who seems to be telling a kid smoking's OK, or even cool? Major corporations like Panasonic and Kellogg's, the local mom-and-pop candy store, the supermarket, the pharmacy, the gas station, the bus company, his doctor, the entire publishing industry, his favorite sports figures, his movie idols, and even his own mother and father.

These things do not go unnoticed.

It seems nobody in the world has a problem with cigarettes except a few teachers and government bureaucrats. Then really, what's the big deal??

This acceptance—this co-option of vast segments of society into the hawking of cigarettes, and most especially this deafening silence—is what is being bought today with the industry's $6 billion-a-year gale-force blizzard of advertising and promotion.

And no once-a-month smoking education class or a few newspaper articles stands a snowball's chance in hell against it.

HOLLYWOOD GLAMORIZES SMOKING

Hillary R. Clinton

> Major motion pictures often include lead characters who make smoking cigarettes and cigars seem like a glamorous, romantic, or powerful activity, writes Hillary R. Clinton in the following selection. The smoking that occurs in movies heightens its allure among young people, she argues, thereby increasing the chances that they will begin to smoke. Given the recent rise in teen smoking, the film industry should recognize its powerful influence on impressionable youth and stop glamorizing cigarettes, Clinton concludes. Clinton, who became First Lady of the United States in 1993, is an attorney who has been active in child welfare and health care issues.

Not long ago, I saw the romantic comedy *My Best Friend's Wedding*. It had a clever plot, witty lines and some unusual high jinks. It also featured a prop increasingly favored in Hollywood movies: the cigarette.

In the film, Julia Roberts, portraying a beautiful and successful career woman, smokes when she's upset. She smokes when she's tired. She smokes when she's happy. In fact, she seems to smoke throughout the movie.

This portrayal of a modern woman so reliant on cigarettes is particularly troubling given that more young women are taking up the deadly habit. The movie only adds to smoking's allure.

Smoking in Movies Is on the Rise

Whether blatant or subtle, smoking in movies is on the rise, sending a confusing message to young people about the use of tobacco products. In 1996, 77 percent of all major motion pictures portrayed the use of tobacco. And in most of those movies, it was the lead actors and actresses who smoked. Every single movie nominated for a 1996 Academy Award in the categories of best picture, best actor and best actress featured tobacco use by a leading character.

These are the findings of Thumbs Up! Thumbs Down!, a project sponsored by the American Lung Association of Sacramento–Emigrant Trails, in which more than 100 teenagers spent a year reviewing current movies to gauge the prevalence of tobacco use.

Reprinted from "Tools of the Tobacco Industry," by Hillary R. Clinton, *Liberal Opinion Week*, August 11, 1997, by permission of Hillary R. Clinton and Creators Syndicate.

These findings are bad news for our nation's children, and they should send a wake-up call to Hollywood studios to acknowledge the influence they wield in our children's lives. Just when the tobacco industry is being held accountable for advertising targeted at young people, movies are stepping in as a powerful vehicle promoting tobacco interests.

The Wrong Messages

As any parent knows, children are often swayed by popular culture. During adolescence, when they are struggling to define who they are and what they want to be, they are bombarded with messages about everything from what they should wear, to how they should look, to ways they should act.

Movie stars who puff away on the screen equate smoking with status, power, confidence and glamour. That's why a dynamic woman smoking throughout *My Best Friend's Wedding*, an intelligent scientist lighting up in *Contact* and Leonardo DiCaprio playing a chain-smoking Romeo in *Romeo and Juliet* send children the wrong message.

Perhaps not surprisingly, cigarette smoking is increasing among American teens, despite the best efforts of parents and teachers to educate children about the dangerous effects of tobacco. Between 1991 and 1995, the percentage of eighth- and tenth-graders who smoked jumped by more than one-third.

And it's not just cigarettes that are attracting children these days. Cigar use is growing among adults—and kids, too—thanks in part to marketing strategies that have given the cigar new cachet as an emblem of wealth and sophistication. More than one in four children between the ages of 14 and 19 smoked a cigar in 1996, according to a study released by the Robert Wood Johnson Foundation in 1997.

Sadly, there seems to be a perception that cigars are not as dangerous as cigarettes. In fact, research has shown that cigar smokers are at a greater risk than nonsmokers of contracting tongue, throat and lung cancer and suffering from strokes and heart attacks. Also worrisome are the health effects on those exposed to secondhand cigar smoke.

A National Priority

The statistics are troubling because nine out of 10 adult smokers begin before they are 18. Once they take up the habit, they're often hooked for life.

That's why reducing smoking among young people must remain a national priority. For the past several years, the President and his Administration have pushed for tougher restrictions on tobacco sales to and advertising aimed at children.

Now, leaders of the motion-picture industry need to join the campaign. Instead of hiding behind the excuse of artistic license, they should admit that most film scenes depicting smoking are gratuitous—whether it's Will Smith celebrating every triumph by lighting a cigar in *Independence Day* or Kurt Russell unveiling a pack of red, white and blue cigarillos with the brand name "Freedom" in *Escape from L.A.*

Rather than allow themselves to be tools of the tobacco industry, they should follow the example of the nurse Hannah in *The English Patient.*

"Can you get me a cigarette?" the patient asks Hannah after his plane has been shot down in World War II.

"Are you crazy?" she replies.

That should be everyone's response to smoking—including those who make and star in Hollywood movies.

YOUNG BLACKS LINK TOBACCO USE TO MARIJUANA

Jane Gross

New York Times writer Jane Gross reports that although a variety of factors play a role in the increase in teen smoking, researchers have discovered a less obvious contributor to tobacco smoking among black youth: marijuana use. In interviews and surveys, many African American teen smokers claim that they started smoking cigarettes after they discovered that nicotine enhances a marijuana high. Moreover, she writes, because of the increasing popularity of marijuana among black teens, marijuana often serves as a "gateway drug" to cigarettes among African American youth.

In the search to explain the spike in smoking among black teen-agers, a range of theories has evolved, from the proliferation of tobacco advertising in minority communities to the stress of adolescence to the identification with entertainment idols who appear with cigarettes dangling from their lips.

Teen-agers themselves, and some experts who have studied adolescent smoking, add another, less predictable explanation to the mix of factors: the decision to take up smoking because of a belief that cigarettes prolong the heady rush of marijuana.

"It makes the high go higher," said Marquette, a 16-year-old student at Saunders Trades and Technical High School in Yonkers, New York, who, like other students, spoke about her marijuana use on the condition that only her first name be used.

At Washington Preparatory High School in South-Central Los Angeles, Tifanni, also 16, said she took up cigarettes in the previous two months because, "If the marijuana goes down and you get a cigarette, it will go up again."

Cigarettes and Marijuana

Black teen-agers like Marquette and Tifanni are not unusual, according to interviews with dozens of adolescents around the country and various national surveys. These surveys show that blacks begin smoking cigarettes later than white teen-agers, but start using marijuana earlier, a difference that experts say they cannot explain.

The surveys also show a sharp rise in both cigarette and marijuana use among teen-agers in recent years, evident among all races but most pronounced among blacks. White teen-agers still smoke cigarettes at twice the rate of blacks, but the gap is narrowing, signaling the end of low smoking rates among black youths that had been considered a public health success story.

It is not clear how much of the increase in smoking among black teen-agers is due to the use of cigarettes with marijuana, and experts say advertising has been the main factor. But the marijuana-tobacco combination is notable because it is the reverse of the more common progression from cigarette and alcohol use to illegal drugs.

Many black teen-agers said in interviews that they were drawn to cigarettes by friends who told them that nicotine would enhance their high from marijuana, which has been lore and practice among drug users of all races for decades. And this is apparently no mere myth. Many scientists who study brain chemistry say the link between cigarettes and marijuana is unproven but likely true.

"African-American youth talk very explicitly about using smoking to maintain a high," said Robin Mermelstein, a professor at the University of Illinois at Chicago and the principal investigator in an ongoing study of why teen-agers smoke for the Federal Centers for Disease Control and Prevention. "It's a commonly stated motivator."

Dr. Mermelstein said that in focus groups with 1,200 teen-agers around the country, about half the blacks mentioned taking up cigarettes to enhance a marijuana high, but no white teen-agers volunteered that as an explanation for smoking. "Cigarettes have a totally different functional value for black and white kids," she said.

Media Messages Are a Factor

Even so, Dr. Mermelstein and others say that does not diminish the greater impact of advertising and other media messages in minority neighborhoods. "Kids are extraordinarily aware of the entertainment media," Dr. Mermelstein said. "They are very reluctant to see the link between any of these and their behavior. But the influence is undoubtedly there."

Tiffany Faulkner, a 15-year-old at Ida B. Wells High School in Jamaica, Queens, said, "Tupac smoked and he's my man," referring to the slain rap star Tupac Shakur. "But I didn't smoke because of him," she said. "I have my own head."

Brand loyalty, however, suggests youths are more moved by the advertising than they realize, or are willing to admit. In general, Marlboro and Camel have white characters on billboards and are the brands of choice among white teen-agers, while Kool and Newport use minority images and are favored by African-Americans teen-agers, as they are by their parents. Outside Brighton High School in Boston, for instance, every black student in a group of smokers chose New-ports. "They're the cool cigarette," said Joey Simone, 18, a smoker since she was 11.

A 16-year-old Chicago girl who tried cigarettes briefly, said she is certain advertising is the key. "When I was little I would see pictures of people standing around with a cigarette and it looked like fun," said Coleco Davis at DuSable High School. "They were all having a good time and it didn't look like it could hurt you."

Researchers Are Worried

This wave of new black smokers, drawn to a habit that kills more people each year than all illegal drugs combined, has researchers wor-ried, because once teen-agers have experienced the booster rocket effect of cigarettes prolonging a marijuana high they often find them-selves addicted to tobacco.

"Because I was getting high, I needed it," said Mary, 16, a student at Norman Thomas High School in Manhattan. "The cigarettes made me more high. Now it's become a habit. I feel bad because there's nothing I can do to stop."

The concern about teen-age smoking is behind pending Federal legislation that would raise the price of cigarettes, control advertising to young people and penalize manufacturers if there is not a gradual reduction in adolescent smoking. That legislation took center stage in Washington just as a study in April 1998 showed a steep rise in the smoking rate among black youths.

The nationwide Federal study showed overall smoking rates had increased by one third among high school students between 1991 and 1997. Most alarming to experts was the sharp rise among black youths: 22.7 percent in 1997, up from 12.6 percent six years earlier.

The "Reverse Gateway Effect"

Charyn Sutton, whose Philadelphia marketing company conducts focus groups for Federal research agencies, said she first heard about the current progression from marijuana to cigarettes—what she calls the "reverse gateway effect"—during focus groups in 1995 involving black middle school students. Ms. Sutton already knew about blunts, cigars hollowed of tobacco and filled with marijuana. But now the teen-agers told her that a practice familiar to the drug cognoscenti as early as the 1960's and 1970's was popular in the schoolyard of the late 1990's—enhancing the high of a joint with a cigarette.

She tested what the teen-agers told her by talking to addicts in recovery, who concurred. And to be sure that the pattern she was see-ing in Philadelphia was not a local anomaly, she interviewed young blacks across the nation. She discovered that they were doing the same thing.

The enhancing effect that teen-agers describe is consistent with what is already known about the working of nicotine and THC, the active ingredient in marijuana. Both spur production of dopamine, a brain chemical that produces pleasurable sensations, said George Koob, a professor of neuro-pharmacology at the Scripps Research Institute in La Jolla, Calif. "It makes a lot of sense," Dr. Koob said.

At the National Institute on Drug Abuse, which funds most of the world's research on addiction, Alan I. Lesher, the director, went a step further, saying the anecdotal findings cried out for rigorous investigation. "This is a reasonable scientific question," he said. "And if enough people report experiencing it, it merits consideration."

Researchers elsewhere have also taken note of strange glitches in substance abuse data comparing blacks and whites. For instance, Denise Kandel, a professor of public health and psychology at Columbia University's College of Physicians and Surgeons, found that while most substance abusers progressed logically from legal to illegal substances, "the pattern of progression is less regular among blacks and nobody really knows why."

Troubling Statistics

In 1991, according to the Centers for Disease Control and Prevention, 14.7 percent of students said they had used marijuana in the last 30 days. By 1995, the latest year for which data is available, that rate had jumped to 25.3 percent. Among white youths, the rate increased to 24.6 percent from 15.2. Among Hispanics, it shot up to 27.8 from 14.4 and among blacks to 28.8 from 13.5, vaulting them from last place to first in marijuana use by racial group.

The C.D.C. cigarette study, which tracks use through 1997, shows a parallel pattern. Among white students, 39.7 percent said they smoked cigarettes, up from 30.9 percent six years ago. Among Hispanic students, more than one third now say they smoke, up from roughly a quarter. Among black youths, 22.7 percent list themselves as smokers, compared with the 12.6 who said they smoked in 1991. Worst of all were the smoking rates for black males, which doubled in the course of the study, to 28.2 from 14.1.

The progression from marijuana to cigarettes among black youths was the most provocative finding in interviews in recent days with high school students in New York City, its suburbs, Los Angeles, Chicago and Boston, who consistently raised the issue without being asked. But their comments raised several other troubling issues, as well.

The students were perfectly aware of the health hazards of cigarette smoking. A 17-year-old at Norman Thomas High School in Manhattan said she was quitting because she might be pregnant. A 15-year-old at Saunders said she did not smoke during basketball and softball season but resumed in between.

But most paid no mind to the danger. And despite laws prohibiting sales to anyone under 18, virtually all the teen-agers said they had no trouble purchasing cigarettes.

The Federal legislation to curb teen-age smoking depends in large measure on steep price increases as a deterrent. Sponsors of the bill say that raising the price by $1.10 per pack would reduce youth smoking by as much as 40 percent. But talking to high school students suggests this prediction is optimistic. [This federal antismoking bill failed in June 1998. As of March 1999, a federal lawsuit was pending.]

The adolescents said overwhelmingly that they would pay $3.60 a pack—the current $2.50 charged in New York plus the additional $1.10 envisioned in the legislation. A few said that $5 a pack might inspire them to quit, or at least to try.

But faced with that high a tariff, 17-year-old Robert Reid, a student in Yonkers, had another idea. "At that price," he said, "you might as well buy weed."

Peer Pressure Causes Teens to Smoke

Jamie Penn

Alexandria, Virginia, high school student Jamie Penn participated in a teen panel that testified before a congressional committee during the 1998 hearings about the settlement between forty-six states and four major tobacco companies. The following selection is taken from Penn's testimony, in which he argues that teen smoking is the result of peer pressure and family influences. He contends, furthermore, that teen smokers cannot simply be labeled as rebellious types; athletes and honor society members are just as likely to smoke as any other youth. Most teens smoke to fit in and to impress others by appearing sophisticated and reckless, Penn maintains.

I went around my school and asked random friends who smoke why they do. Nine out of ten responded that it was simply peer pressure. I do not mean the clichéd after-school special, health video, public service announcement, "Hey man, everybody's doing it," type of peer pressure.

When you see your friends and parents lighting up, it has a powerful impact. At that point, any anti-smoking propaganda that you have digested is completely forgotten. When a child grows up in a smoking environment, they tend to wind up having the worst addiction.

Wendy, a friend of mine, has parents like that. They would buy her cartons and cartons of cigarettes. What kind of a message is this sending? How can parents one minute tell their kid not to smoke when the next minute they are nearly hacking up a lung, finishing off that third pack of the day?

It is sort of funny when one of my friends, Eric, comes to me one day in school and says, "Oh man, I just got busted by my parents last night for smoking. I am grounded for two weeks." A month later he gets busted again by the school for smoking on school grounds.

The parents look the other way because it is a lost cause. He is already addicted.

Reprinted from Jamie Penn's testimony before the U.S. House Committee on Commerce, Subcommittee on Health and the Environment, March 19, 1998.

Teen Smokers Cannot Be Pigeonholed

The first thing that this [congressional] committee needs to realize is that the vast majority of teens have smoked at least once or twice and many of those smoke on a regular basis. Teen smokers of today can no longer be pigeonholed as the rebellious punks that lurk in dark alleys.

They are not the jocks, the artists, the preps, the musicians, the skaters, the nerds, the intellects, and the rebellious punks. Go to any trendy coffee shop and you will barely be able to see through the thick cloud of cigarette smoke that blankets the room.

The kids that are so earnestly discussing philosophy and international affairs are in the meantime puffing on the cigarettes that they know to be dangerous. Why are these otherwise smart kids doing something so moronic? Because of the impression it gives.

There is a certain laidback vibe to smoking that we love. Nothing combats emotional weariness like a feeling of reckless abandon (i.e., smoking). [Take the story of] a friend of mine, Kyle, who was a freshman the same year his older brother was a senior.

In order to fit in, Kyle followed his brother to parties and picked up the habit of smoking because it made him feel like he belonged. This year as a senior, he is a National Honor Society member with a schedule full of Advanced Placement courses and varsity sports.

Not exactly the image you would expect of a chain smoker. Once addicted, my friends make up any excuse to get away and take that drag that they so desperately need. How many cigarette breaks does it take during their homework? How many times do they have to take their dogs for a walk?

I have noticed that in my school, the ones that take those drags to fit in are the first ones to incorporate marijuana and alcohol into their social routine. Remember my friend Kyle? Well, he is a pothead too.

Youths Need Education

During the years of health education I received regarding the dangers of smoking, the one thing that I remember now and will never forget was the video about the effects.

We talk of emphysema and we talk of cancer, but until you see it, you do not understood the significance. In one such video, there was a man who smoked his entire life, starting at the tender age of seven and continuing on until his final days. Through the entire interview he smoked through a hole in his trachea.

America was founded on the primary belief of freedom of choice. People have always been given the choice to smoke or not. That is why I feel that the money that would change hands through this [tobacco] settlement should not go to assist those with diseases brought on by tobacco, but to educating the youth on how stupid it is to start this fatal habit.

TEENS SMOKE TO SEEM GROWN-UP

Kaz Vorpal

Adolescents often try to prove that they are "cool" by engaging in what society considers to be adult activity. Emphasizing that smoking is only for adults, then, makes cigarettes more attractive to teenagers, argues Kaz Vorpal in the following selection. The implication that mature men and women can make the decision to smoke is a more significant factor in the increase in teen smoking than are cigarette ads and peer pressure, he contends. Vorpal is a website developer who lives near Washington, D.C.

Teen smoking is on the rise. Hugely on the rise.
   What could be causing this?
   Peer pressure? Peer pressure is nothing new. Something is causing an *increase*, so it must be something that is actually changing.
   Could it really be that Joe Camel causes this, even though Camel is one of the brands teens smoke least? [Joe Camel was a cartoon character created for Camel cigarette ads. These ads were discontinued in 1997.] Why are they smoking so many Marlboros, despite the very grown-up advertisements?

Becoming "Adult"

There is another reason that is surely at least part of the cause:
   Ask yourself what motivates children, especially teenagers, to do things that are harmful to themselves, and one of the first major answers is that they are trying to become like, or prove they are, adults.
   Adults do certain things, and therefore children who do those things feel they are more like grownups.
   Women wear high heels and makeup. Children really aren't supposed to. So little girls (we're not going to complicate this with sex identity debate, as that's not the point here) play dress-up, and teenage girls often want to wear more makeup, higher heels, and more "adult" clothing than their mothers think should be seen on any human of any age. . . .
   Boys tend to do the same, using the macho model . . . cuss, play sports, drink, shoot guns. . . .

Reprinted, with permission, from "Who Is Causing So Much Teen Smoking?" by Kaz Vorpal. Web article published at www.smart.net/~kaz/tobacco.html.

This was, obviously, McDonald's theory behind their Arch Deluxe ad campaign. Remember it? "Children just hate our sandwiches, only *grownups* like them! This is a sandwich for *adults*!"

Now, if McDonald's *really* believed that, would they have spent their entire ad budget talking about it, instead of targeting the people who would actually EAT it? Of course not . . . and they *were* targeting the people they wanted to get to eat it . . . the kids like the ones in the commercials.

Raise your hand if you believe they spent their entire ad campaign promoting how people *really* didn't like their sandwich. . . .

Boys and Girls Do Not Smoke

Now, what has the government, who teaches children that it is an authority on pretty much all things, been telling everyone, especially children?

- Smoking is for Grownups
- Only Adults Should Smoke Cigarettes
- Mere Children Should Not Smoke; Only Mature People Get That Choice
- Men Smoke, Women Smoke, Little Boys and Girls Do Not

Now what, exactly, is the impression that children are getting from this?

Maybe tons of makeup or a good gun isn't enough, eh?

REAL grownups, of course, are allowed to smoke.

Perhaps the real cause of the rise in teen smoking in the United States is not the tobacco companies . . . perhaps it is, as is often the case, the people who want power and money and say it's because they're protecting children. . . .

No wonder the tobacco companies say they're all for an ad campaign to keep children away from smoking . . . that would have the same effect the government's campaign to get kids away from tobacco has had for the last several years—increasing teen smoking. . . .

I say this as a non-smoker, who believes that smoking is a mistake, and is certainly one kids should not even consider making. But this does not mean that we should do things which make us feel better because they sound like they would help, but in reality will only make things worse.

Prohibition does not work, even if it were "right" to ban others from doing things we do not like. Prohibition causes more of the very problems we want to prevent. It has the opposite effect of the reason we would consider imposing it in the first place.

Individuals Are Responsible for Choosing to Smoke

Jay Ambrose

Jay Ambrose is chief editorial writer for Scripps Howard News Service. In the following piece, he contends that young people themselves are responsible for making the decision to smoke. People choose to smoke even when they are fully informed of tobacco's dangers, he points out, so only they are accountable for the consequences of their choice. Those who blame tobacco companies and cigarette ads for illnesses caused by smoking are perpetuating a "victim mentality" that denies the importance of individual choice and accountability, Ambrose maintains.

Said the young man, puff, puff, it's the fault of the tobacco companies. They, deep drag, conspired to addict me. Someday the courts should force them to pay me and pay me a lot. Smoke curled around his head.

My reply went something like this:

Yes, maybe at least some of the tobacco companies did all they could to enhance the addictive qualities of cigarettes, knowing full well those same cigarettes can kill.

And it's true nicotine can grab hold of you with a python-like grip. In his autobiography, Ray Charles said it was harder for him to quit smoking than it was to give up heroin.

Smokers Know the Dangers

But when you put that first cigarette in your mouth, when you first inhaled the smoke deep in your lungs, you knew the dangers.

The cigarette packages themselves tell you their contents are deadly, and people have preached that message to you from virtually the day you were born. Even if the surgeon general had never produced evidence of smoking as a cause of cancer and heart disease, common sense would have told you that sucking an irritant into your lungs could scarcely be a good idea.

You also knew that very few people, once they have launched their smoking careers, can give up cigarettes without a struggle. Almost

Reprinted, with permission, from "Where Smoking Blame Belongs," by Jay Ambrose, *The Washington Times*, February 14, 1996.

always they work their way up to a pack a day, or two packs or three packs. That's simple observation.

Certainly, the cigarette companies tempted you. In advertisements, they made smoking look manly and sophisticated. But life is full of temptations to do things we know are bad for us. No one pointed a gun at your head. The choice was yours. What is more, every time you light up a cigarette the choice is yours. You really don't have to do it.

Addiction comes down to this: You feel uncomfortable, perhaps to the point of distress, if you don't indulge the habit. But people can endure discomfort when they know the habit will result in a shortened life and perhaps a painful death, not to mention less vigor and damaged health in the intervening years.

Thousands of people have done just that. They have quit smoking. Despite the undeniable urge, they have exercised their free will.

Were the tobacco companies morally right in what they did? Of course they weren't. It's not so clear they did anything illegal, however, and smokers are responsible for their own actions as long as they knew what they were doing when they started and acted of their own volition.

The Issue of Self-Accountability

What worries me is not just the issue of smoking. It's the issue of self-accountability. If you give up thinking you are responsible for your own actions, you are telling a lie to yourself and making it less likely you will ever have the character to become captain of your fate. You also are helping pave the way for an all-intrusive, Big Brother government and for absurd and unworkable criteria for conducting societal affairs.

Too many people in this great land seem caught up in self-exculpatory thinking these days. You see it in people excusing themselves for bad behavior because they were mistreated in some fashion by their parents. What they have apparently missed is all the other people who don't behave that way even though they were subjected to the same sort of mistakes in their upbringing.

You see this sort of thinking in people demanding things they haven't earned because they see themselves as victims. Even if they were cheated of some opportunities in some part of their lives, the best opportunity of the moment is self-rescue. They are victims, all right. They are victims of themselves. They are defeating themselves by waiting around for someone to change their lives.

And you see an absence of responsibility for self in the endless lawsuits to recover damages for what people in fact did to themselves. The next thing you know, fat people with bad hearts will be suing farmers for making food too tasty.

Well, the young man answered, the farmers didn't slip cocaine into

their potatoes, and besides, while you may have stopped smoking cigarettes, you still smoke a pipe.

He had a point about the pipe.

I can only claim I never blamed a tobacco company or a mother
who weaned me too soon.

Nevertheless, mea culpa [I am to blame].

It's better to lead by example than by lecture.

CIGARETTE PROMOTIONAL ITEMS MAY FOSTER TEEN SMOKING

Terence Monmaney

A study published in 1997 links cigarette promotional merchandise with youth smoking, reports Terence Monmaney in the following piece. He points out that youths often acquire this merchandise—including T-shirts and hats sporting cigarette brand names—with cigarette pack coupons. Moreover, the study reveals, teens who own tobacco promotional items are much more likely to smoke than those who do not own such items. Tobacco company spokespersons as well as researchers contend that the study does not ultimately prove that cigarette promotional items encourage teens to smoke, notes Monmaney. However, he writes, many researchers have concluded that this merchandise does increase the chances that younger children will experiment with smoking. Monmaney is a medical writer for the *Los Angeles Times*.

Schoolkids who sport clothing and gear emblazoned with cigarette names and logos are four times more likely to smoke than other children, according to a study suggesting that such promotional items may foster youth smoking.

Although tobacco companies are not allowed by federal regulations to sell or give cigarette-related merchandise to people under 18, children still end up with hats, T-shirts, backpacks and other gear displaying cigarette brand names and trademarks.

Public health experts and anti-smoking advocates have sharply criticized the promotions, saying the items might function as a sort of stealth advertising that interests children in smoking.

In recent years, the tobacco industry has boosted spending on merchandise giveaways and catalog sales, from $307 million in 1990 to $665 million in 1995, according to the most recent Federal Trade Commission (FTC) records. Additional hundreds of millions have been invested annually in items sold at retail stores or "purchased" with cigarette pack coupons.

Meanwhile, national youth smoking rates have risen 1% to 2%

annually since 1992. In 1996, it was estimated that 34% of 12th-graders smoked.

Linking Cigarette Merchandise and Teen Smoking

The study, which is the largest to test the correlation between smoking rates and ownership of cigarette merchandise among public school students, was based on a survey of 1,265 youngsters in grades six through 12 at five facilities in rural Vermont and New Hampshire. It found that the merchandise was substantially more prevalent, and more tightly linked with lighting up, than researchers previously observed.

The researchers found that 32% of the youngsters surveyed owned promotional merchandise. T-shirts and hats were the most common items, Marlboro and Camel the most popular brands. Most of the items came from parents or adult friends, but 22% of the children with an item said that stores or cigarette company catalogs sold it to them directly, in violation of federal laws.

Moreover, 4.8% of the children said they had a promotional item with them on the day of the survey, in October 1996. And because the results indicated that each item taken to school was seen by 10 other youngsters, the findings "raised the possibility that children were becoming the means through which cigarettes were being promoted to other children," wrote the physician-researchers, who are based at Dartmouth Medical School in Hanover, N.H., and the Veterans Affairs Medical Center in White River Junction, Vt.

A youngster was more likely to smoke if he or she owned a promotional item, the researchers say. Among the 12th-graders, 32% overall were classified as smokers, meaning they admitted to having smoked more than 100 cigarettes. But 58% of those who owned a promotional item smoked, compared to 23% of those who did not own one.

The association was strongest in the lower grades, which especially concerned the researchers because that is when crucial attitudes toward smoking are being formed. Only 3% of sixth-graders were classified as smokers, but all of them said they owned a promotional item.

"This is the most powerful demonstration yet that these promotional items have a disproportionate impact on kids," said Matthew Myers, executive vice president of the National Center for Tobacco Free Kids.

Other Factors Can Contribute to Smoking

Tobacco company spokespersons disputed the findings, which were made public in December 1997 in an American Medical Association journal, the *Archives of Pediatric and Adolescent Medicine*.

The study also uncovered strong evidence of family and peer pressure on smoking trends: The likelihood that youngsters smoked was boosted nearly seven times if they had friends who did so, and 28 times if both friends and family members smoked.

The lead author, Dartmouth pediatrician Dr. James Sargent, said that a survey cannot prove that the promotional items caused the children to start smoking. Still, he said the results clearly show that the merchandise appears to put very young children at greater risk of experimenting with cigarettes.

John Pierce, a cancer prevention expert at the University of California in San Diego who has studied cigarette advertisements' effect on children, said he was impressed that about a third of the youngsters in the study had promotional items. In a random telephone survey of California residents in 1993, Pierce and his co-workers found that 9% of people of high school age had such an item. "If it was a problem [then], it's a much bigger problem now," he said.

Does the Research Prove Causality?

Tobacco companies pointed out that cigarette promotional items were around long before the recent increase in youth smoking. Peggy Carter, a spokeswoman for R.J. Reynolds, maker of Camel, said the "bottom line" was that the research did not establish causality.

Beyond that, she said, the company takes numerous steps to prevent minors from purchasing company merchandising. Catalog orders require a signature attesting that a customer is over 21, and the company uses five databases to protect against fraud, including motor vehicle and voter registries, she said.

"We wish that parents would not tolerate their children having items associated with our brands," she said. "We think it's inappropriate. But that's an issue between parents and children.". . .

In suggesting the link between promotional items and youth smoking, the study appears to overstate the growth of tobacco industry spending on the items. It says that such spending went from $310 million in 1990 to $1.25 billion in 1994—a fourfold increase. But the earlier figure does not include promotional coupons redeemed for cigarettes in addition to merchandise, whereas the more recent spending figure does.

The FTC reports that combined merchandising and cigarette-promotion totals were $1.49 billion in 1990 and $2.1 billion in 1994—a 41% increase.

TOBACCO PROMOTIONAL ITEMS DO NOT CAUSE TEEN SMOKING

Jacob Sullum

Tobacco promotional items such as jackets with cigarette logos are usually obtained by sending in proofs-of-purchase to a cigarette manufacturer. Research has revealed that teens who own tobacco-related merchandise are more likely to smoke than teens who do not own such items. This information has led many commentators to conclude that cigarette promotional items (CPIs) encourage teen smoking. In the following selection, Jacob Sullum takes issue with this stance, arguing that research has not proven that the desire for CPIs actually causes teens to start smoking. It may be that young people who acquire such merchandise do so after they have already become smokers, he points out. Sullum is the senior editor of *Reason* magazine and the author of *For Your Own Good: The Anti-Smoking Crusade and the Tyranny of Public Health.*

Probably the most important thing I picked up from all those psychology courses I took in college can be summed up in four words: Correlation is not causation. As *Basic Psychology* put it, "The fact that two variables are correlated says nothing about the underlying causal relationship between them." It's a lesson that many journalists have yet to learn.

Consider how the press covered a a study reported in December 1997 in *Archives of Pediatric and Adolescent Medicine.* The researchers surveyed about 1,200 students in grades six through 12 and found that kids who owned cigarette promotional items such as jackets and backpacks were four times as likely to smoke as those who did not. It hardly seems surprising that owners of tobacco-related merchandise tend to be smokers, and this fact alone tells us nothing about why people smoke.

Shoddy Logic

Yet newspaper coverage portrayed the survey results as evidence that kids smoke *because of* promotional merchandise. "Tobacco Gear a Big

From "Smoking Jackets," by Jacob Sullum, *Reason Online*, December 24, 1997, published at www.reason.com. Reprinted by permission of Jacob Sullum and Creators Syndicate.

Draw for Kids," announced the headline in the *Boston Globe*. The story began, "If tobacco manufacturers hope to promote smoking by producing clothing or accessories emblazoned with cigarette logos, research by Dartmouth Medical School suggests that the tactic works well."

Under the headline, "Study: Logos Foster Smoking," *Newsday* reported that "children who own cigarette promotional items . . . are far more likely to smoke." The story did not note that this observation is open to more than one interpretation, but it did quote the lead researcher, James D. Sargent, who said, "We found that, in effect, children are being used to market cigarettes to their peers."

The *Los Angeles Times* headline was more cautious: "Study Links Cigarette Gear, Youth Smoking." The lead said, "Schoolkids who sport clothing and gear emblazoned with cigarette names and logos are four times more likely to smoke than other children, according to a new study suggesting that such promotional items may foster youth smoking." The reporter waited until the 14th paragraph to tell us that Sargent admitted "a survey cannot prove that the promotional items caused the children to start smoking."

A rather important point, you might think. Yet all of the stories I saw either ignored or downplayed it. The *Globe*, for instance, quoted Sargent's complaint that "the tobacco industry is always going to question the causality. That's pretty much what they did with the link between cigarette smoking and cancer."

Sargent thus suggested that only self-interested nitpickers would be so bold as to point out the glaring weakness in his study. Yet he and his colleagues themselves conceded, "The finding of an association between CPI [cigarette promotional item] ownership and being a smoker could easily be an expression of an adolescent who acquired these items after having made the decision to become a smoker." Not to put too fine a point on it, but *duh*.

A Cause-and-Effect Relationship?

Later in the article, Sargent et al. wrote, "Our study and others published to date are subject to the usual limitations inherent in cross-sectional studies, in that we are unable to infer a direction between the exposure (ownership of a CPI) and smoking behavior, limiting our ability to invoke a causal relationship between CPI ownership and smoking." Translation: We would like to say that promotional items make kids smoke, but this study doesn't show that.

The researchers did not let that quibble get in the way of their policy recommendation: "All CPI distribution should end immediately." And in case you missed the point, an editor's note in a box at the beginning of the article said: "If CPIs were bacteria, no one would be opposed to eradication. So why can't we eliminate this pathogen?"

Cigarette promotional items, of course, aren't bacteria. They are a form of speech that offends many people—including, apparently, the

researchers who did this study and the editor of the journal that published it.

In this country, however, we do not usually ban speech just
because it's offensive. The purpose of studies like this one is to convince people that Marlboro caps and Joe Camel T-shirts are somehow
worse than racist fulminations, flag burning, nude dancing, pornogra-
phy, and sacrilegious art. That's a tall order, so it helps to have a cred-
ulous audience that does not remember much from Psych 101.

CHAPTER 3

PERSPECTIVES ON SMOKING

Contemporary Issues
Companion

LETTER TO A YOUNG SMOKER

Anna Quindlen

The following piece consists of an open letter written by nationally syndicated columnist Anna Quindlen to the seventeen-year-old daughter of Quindlen's friend, imploring her to give up cigarettes. The author urges the young woman to consider the many ways in which she is endangering her health and her future by smoking. Quindlen also cites the example of a once-successful model, Janet Sackman, who lost her larynx and part of a lung as a result of the smoking habit she acquired at age seventeen. Although Quindlen realizes that every person—whether a teenager or an adult—must come to an individual decision about smoking, she hopes that her letter will help persuade her friend's daughter to stop smoking.

Dear Golden Girl,

Got a letter from your mom the other day. Her description did you proud: "At seventeen she is at the high end of meeting every parent's expectations, including mine," she wrote. "An A student, captain of the tennis team, president of her high school service organization."

But her tone was despondent, disappointed and angry. You've started to smoke, and she wants me to persuade you to stop.

That's not the way it works. Seventeen or 70, people quit smoking when they've convinced themselves it's the right thing to do. But there are a couple of things I can mention.

Picture the Future

There's the guy you may fall in love with someday who thinks kissing a smoker is as seductive as licking the bottom of a dirty ashtray. There are the babies you might want to have and the damage you could do to them in utero if you are so addicted to cigarettes that you can't quit when you're pregnant.

There are the yellow fingers and the yellow teeth. Your clothes smell. So does your hair. It gets harder to stop every day.

In this very newspaper [the New York Times] we ran a photograph of two fashion industry types wearing T-shirts that are part of a campaign to combat breast cancer. They were holding bottles of designer water in one hand and cigarettes in the other. The mixed messages you receive are confusing.

There's nothing confusing about smoking for me. I remember the day of the rehearsal dinner for Jim and Mary's wedding, when my father-in-law picked me up at the bus stop, his voice whittled away to a faint rasp. A cold, he said. Laryngitis. A year later he was dead of lung cancer, still smoking up to the end.

Bill Cahan, the surgeon who has been an inveterate opponent of the tobacco industry, sent me a photograph of a diseased lung. It looks like an alien life form in a bad sci-fi movie. He says I should remind you that smokers who take the pill face an increased risk of hardening of the arteries, stroke and heart disease, and that tongue cancer is on the rise.

Joe Cherner, who founded an anti-smoking advocacy group, says I should mention that you're being manipulated by the middle-aged. "There's an entire group of adults whose careers depend on getting you to start smoking by deception," he says. More than 400,000 people will die because of cigarettes each year. You're part of the next wave, the new wave, of consumers, patients, fatalities. Welcome to the oncology floor.

A Young Model's Story

And meet Janet Sackman, who remembers 17 as if it were yesterday.

"When I was 17 I had the world in my hands," she says, and she's not exaggerating. She was a successful model: soap and swimsuit ads, the cover of *Life* and *Look*. In 1949 they stood her on skis in a studio with phony mountains in the background and a fan blowing her blonde hair and made her the Lucky Strike girl. There was just one catch: "An executive for the tobacco people said to me, 'It would be a good idea for you to learn how to smoke. That way you'll look authentic.'"

So at just your age Janet learned to smoke. She went on to do Chesterfield ads on television—"You know, he's right!" she enthused when the announcer said that Chesterfield left no unpleasant after-taste—and to marry and have four children. In 1983 she had her larynx removed and in 1990 she lost part of one lung.

She still looks great but she doesn't sound so good. Her voice box gone, she had to learn to talk all over again, burping air through a hole in her esophagus just above the collarbone. It took her about six months to say her first word; now she teaches others the technique.

"I cough through that hole, I sneeze through that hole, and I talk through that hole," she says in a mechanical croak. "I can't make any sound when I laugh or cry. I can't be sarcastic and I can't tell a joke. I have the same monotone speech all the time."

"And I'm one of the fortunate ones," she added, "because I'm alive.

I wish I had realized how important my life was when I was 17. Tell her the single most important thing to do for your looks and your life, the single most important thing, is not to smoke. If she could hear me speak, she'd listen."

Your mother says you have a birthday coming up. Here's Janet Sackman's suggestion for what you could give yourself as a gift: many many more.

I WILL QUIT SMOKING WHEN YOU GIVE UP DRIVING

Ron Tunning

> A smoker since he was fourteen, Ron Tunning writes that he is determined not to give up his cigarette habit. He admits that his resolve to continue smoking is a kind of adolescent rebelliousness that is spurred on by society's efforts to curb smoking. Irritated by laws that ban smoking in public places, Tunning contends that no one should be forced to relinquish a habit simply because others find it deplorable. Tunning is a freelance writer and former developer living in Florence, Kentucky.

My earliest recollection of an attempt on my part to smoke a cigarette reaches back to my pre-school days during the summer of 1956. Our family had only recently moved into a new home in Florence, Kentucky's Greenbriar subdivision, and my eldest brother had swiped a pack of Viceroy from my mom to share with some boys in the neighborhood he was hoping to impress into friendship.

There was an enormous pile of old lumber and debris stacked near the woods which bordered the rear of the subdivision, and my brother decided to use it as fuel for a bonfire, doubting that the three matches he'd brought along would be enough to get us through 20 cigarettes.

I can't recall that any of us ever managed to light one of the "coffin nails" because before we knew it the fire had raged out of control and the volunteer fire department had to be summoned to extinguish the flames. My father was one who believed that to "spare the rod was to spoil the child," so I imagine it was quite some time before we again entertained a notion to smoke.

The First Pack of Cigarettes

My first purchase of a pack of cigarettes occurred when I was 14. Each summer I'd spend several weeks with my grandparents in Akron, Ohio, and my parents had decided I was old enough to travel alone by Greyhound.

When the bus stopped in Washington Court House to pick up passengers, I exited long enough to plunk a quarter in a machine for a pack of BelAir.

Reprinted, with permission, from "I'll Think of Quitting Smoking When You Give Up Driving," by Ron Tunning, *The Cincinnati Post*, June 25, 1998.

Before making it to Mansfield, I'd inhaled enough mentholated tobacco smoke to have created a fog throughout the bus, and I soon discovered that instead of feeling "cool" and terribly grown-up, I was becoming increasingly ill. In fact, I distinctly recall thinking I was about to die, and my desire to be perceived as an adult gave way to a childlike need for parental comfort and reassurance.

Within a couple of years of that trip I'd forgotten the ill side effects and was inhaling a pack of Marlboros per day. By the time I'd graduated from high school and entered college that habit had increased to two daily packs. A subsequent tour in the military inflated consumption to nearly three packs daily, gratefully at commissary prices.

Unlike most of my family and friends, I've yet to abandon the habit. I continue to generate healthy profits for the Philip Morris Tobacco Company, and considerable tax revenue for both the state and federal governments. Admittedly, I've probably spent enough on converting leaves to ash to have funded a small medical center.

Determined to Continue Smoking

One would be reasonable to assume that I should know better than to continue polluting my lungs and the air around me, and to expect that I'd have a greater regard for my health, if not an appropriate consideration for those who must share the secondhand smoke. I suspect that aside from my obvious addiction to nicotine, my reticence about quitting is an indication of a rather adolescent form of rebellion. The more I'm told to quit, and the more adamant society becomes in its efforts to eliminate smoking, the more determined I am to continue.

The recent news reports on non-smokers trying to force the Greater Cincinnati/Northern Kentucky International Airport to eliminate all smoking areas, citing the "Americans with Disabilities Act" as prohibiting smoking in public buildings where those with asthma or other breathing disorders might be bothered by secondhand smoke, has hardened my resolve to continue lighting up, particularly in public places.

My first inclination was to file a countersuit claiming that my nicotine addiction qualifies as a disability, and as such, should be afforded the same accommodation offered to those requiring wheelchair lifts or non-smoking areas. If elevators servicing parking garages are required to provide Braille encoded controls, nicotine addicts should have a space to emit their socially offensive haze.

Having decided, however, that the courts are already inundated with ridiculous lawsuits, I've chosen instead to offer a compromise to those bothered by secondhand smoke. I'll avoid lighting-up in public if they'll park their automobiles.

Think about it for a moment. Would you rather inhale the smoke from my cigarette or be forced to breathe in the exhaust from your automobile? How many people can you recall having committed suicide by locking themselves in a garage and puffing away on a Camel?

I will admit that smoking is unhealthy, unsightly, and a thoroughly disgusting habit. So is cheating on your spouse or wearing spandex unless you have the body of Cindy Crawford. Tattoos and body piercing are viewed as repulsive by many, and drivers with cell phones glued to their ears are dangerous.

But I'm not about to suggest that laws be passed to force people to adhere to my sense of propriety or good taste, nor do I look fondly upon those who do. In so far as I'm concerned, you can eat your Big Macs and shovel pints of Graeter's ice cream into your bulging midriff, or you can parade around in a chartreuse pants suit with spiked hair and a dog collar around your neck if it makes you happy.

And me? I'll be annoying you with my Marlboros, sans the cowboy outfit, unless, of course, you've permanently parked your car.

THE PRICE OF SMOKING

David W. Cowles

David W. Cowles started smoking when he was fifteen in order to appear more sophisticated, and he grew to enjoy the intoxicating effects of nicotine. After fifty years of smoking and several unenthusiastic attempts at quitting, he writes, his declining health finally forced him to give up cigarettes. However, shortly after he stopped smoking, he was diagnosed with emphysema and lung cancer, the legacy of a lifetime of smoking. Despite the fact that he enjoyed smoking, Cowles states that, in retrospect, he wishes he had never started. Cowles is a resident of Las Vegas, Nevada.

I'm not going to waste your time trying to persuade you to quit smoking. You've already heard or read all of the reasons that you shouldn't light up. You've seen the surgeon general's warnings on every pack of cigarettes and in every tobacco ad. You've been lectured by friends and family. You're aware that more people die from lung cancer than from breast cancer, prostate cancer and colorectal cancer combined—and that almost all lung cancer is caused by smoking.

The fact is, until you're ready to break the habit, none of the arguments proffered by antismoking advocates will have even the slightest impact. But, since you've read this far, I'll give you the benefit of my experiences.

I tried my first cigarette when I was 15. Always a scrawny kid, I thought that smoking made me look more adult and sophisticated and therefore more attractive to the opposite sex. Plus, I liked the slightly intoxicated buzz that inhaling provided. Before long, I was hooked and smoking a pack a day.

Fifty years later, I still enjoyed cigarettes. With my morning coffee. After a good meal. Relaxing in front of a video-poker machine at my favorite Las Vegas casino. I'd even joke about nonsmokers, asking what they did after having sex.

My cardiologist tried his best to persuade me to stop. He said I'd reduce the risk of having a heart attack or stroke, lower my blood pressure and improve my circulation. I felt that he was probably right—for other people. After all, my father had smoked all of his life and lived to his 90s. I would listen politely, eager for the good doctor to finish so that I could get out to my car and light up.

On numerous occasions I halfheartedly tried to quit. Not because I really wanted to, but because it seemed to be the right thing to do. Sometimes my determination lasted less than an hour before I absolutely had to have a cigarette.

Much as I didn't want to admit it, for the last couple of years I knew that smoking was affecting my health. I'd be out of breath after climbing a short flight of stairs and had great difficulty keeping pace with my companions in the mile-high air of the Utah mountains where we went trout fishing every Father's Day.

Things got particularly acute this past summer. I'd installed a small fish pond in my backyard, and every week I had to clean out the water filter. Just bending over to open the filter unit wore me out. I'd come back into the house gasping for breath, sit down and smoke several cigarettes until I mustered up the energy to finish the chore.

One night I was on my way home from work when I realized that I was down to three cigarettes. I could stop at a store and buy a carton, or . . . pick up a box of nicotine patches. While I read the instructions, I smoked my last cigarette.

I quickly discovered the two distinct components of the smoking habit: the nicotine addiction and the situational desires. I'll give the patches full credit for alleviating the nervousness and irritability that cold-turkey nicotine withdrawal causes.

The situational aspects of smoking were far more difficult to overcome. When I climbed out of bed, drove off in my car or waited to be served in a restaurant, I automatically reached to my shirt pocket. The smoking habit was deeply entrenched and died very hard indeed.

The results? Within 24 hours, I was not nearly as short of breath. Within days, the morning hacking and spitting up was greatly reduced. At six weeks, I climbed all 91 steps to the top of Kukulkan Pyramid in Chichén Itzá, Mexico.

But 50 years of smoking took their toll. During a routine medical exam last November, my internist determined that I had emphysema. And that wasn't all. An X-ray revealed a spot on one of my lungs. A CAT scan showed it to be a marble-size tumor.

The cardiovascular surgeon postulated that there was a 65 percent chance the tumor was malignant and only 35 percent that it was benign. He recommended an immediate biopsy, with more radical surgery should the tumor prove to be malignant.

I was admitted to the hospital exactly four months from the day I quit smoking. The tumor turned out to be a stage-one squamous cell carcinoma—a type of lung cancer strongly related to smoking. The surgeon removed the tumor and a lobe of one lung.

He told me afterward that I was fortunate. If I had had my physical exam a few months earlier, the tumor might not have been discovered. A few months later, and the cancer might have already spread to the lymph nodes or metastasized elsewhere. The surgeon was confident that all of the cancer had been excised and that there would be no recurrence.

But I felt anything but lucky. For days after the operation I was in such horrendous pain I believed I'd never leave the hospital alive. For more than a month the excruciating pain continued. Even now, I am still very short of breath.

Yes, I genuinely enjoyed smoking. But I certainly wish that I had found my pleasure elsewhere.

THE TESTIMONY OF A TEENAGE TOBACCO FARMER

Jacob Falwell

In the 1990s, dozens of states sued the tobacco industry to recover the costs of treating smoking-related illnesses. In 1998, a settlement was reached in which four tobacco corporations agreed to pay the states $206 billion and to submit to marketing restrictions in an effort to reduce teen smoking. The following excerpt from the March 1998 congressional hearings on the tobacco settlement is taken from the testimony of Jacob Falwell, an eighteen-year-old tobacco farmer and high school student from Murray, Kentucky. Falwell maintains that the tobacco industry provides thousands of jobs and billions of dollars for the U.S. economy. For four generations, he points out, his family has relied on tobacco farming as a significant source of income. A nonsmoker who does not condone teen tobacco use, Falwell argues that the problem of underage smoking originates in the home rather than with the tobacco industry. Instead of creating more governmental restrictions for the tobacco industry, he contends, families should take on the responsibility of curbing teen smoking.

My name is Jacob Falwell. I am an 18-year-old student at Calloway County High School in Murray, Kentucky. I have come [to these congressional hearings on the tobacco settlement] to speak on the heated topic, both in our national, state, and local governments.

This is an issue that I feel very strongly about. Since the days of Christopher Columbus, tobacco has been a part of the land here in North America. Since that time, Americans have become more and more aware of the possibilities tobacco can provide, as well as its economic importance to our country.

I do not smoke, nor do I in any way condone teenage smoking or tobacco use. Smoking is an adult choice to be executed by those who understand the effects and the consequences of tobacco use.

Americans must realize that tobacco provides almost 700,000 individuals with jobs, bringing in an income of almost $15.2 billion. This

Reprinted from Jacob Falwell's testimony before the U.S. House Committee on Commerce, Subcommittee on Health and the Environment, March 19, 1998.

crop even contributed $6 billion toward the U.S. trade balance.

However, the tobacco industry is more than just facts and dollar figures. Of the 150,000 American tobacco farmers, I am one of them. So is my dad. So is my granddad and so was my great-granddad. All on the same plot of land in rural Calloway County, Kentucky. Tobacco was family, four generations strong.

I am just one of the 150,000 other tobacco farmers whose very livelihoods we are debating today. Tobacco is the highest value cash crop with an average value of $4,200 per acre. I have experimented with what you might call an alternative to tobacco.

I have grown up to five acres per year of pumpkins over a four-year span. Throughout those years combined, I received roughly one-fifth the income I could have received from just one acre of tobacco in one year's time.

There is no alternative crop available that can provide such an income for such little acreage. Tobacco generates over 50 percent of the farm income for over 65 percent of the U.S. tobacco farms.

While I receive 100 percent of my yearly income from tobacco while working for my father and uncle on the family row crop farm of 2,100 acres, tobacco is where we make our money. My dad once stated, tobacco is what we live on. It pays the bills. I grow the other crops to run the operation year-round.

The majority of the tobacco farmers in my area supplement their incomes through tobacco production. A neighbor of mine works five days a week in town while his wife is a full-time school teacher.

While working two full-time jobs, the family also raises one acre of dark fired tobacco and 1,300 of burley tobacco. This is not at all uncommon. The amount of work from afternoons and weekends can make enough money to sustain a suitable lifestyle.

Providing for a Future

This May [1998], I plan to set up my fourth crop of tobacco, increasing my acreage from 3.5 acres to 4 acres of dark fired tobacco. Each year that I grow tobacco, I am doing so in order to provide for my future. With tobacco money, I have purchased such things as a vehicle, a personal watercraft and have just recently begun investing in my future through IRAs and mutual funds.

Perhaps the most important use of my tobacco income is going toward college. I plan to attend Murray State University and major in agriculture education, and maybe return to the family farm to continue the historic tradition of raising dark fired tobacco.

I have never received any type of allowance and have never held any other job. However, I am able to do just as my cousins and brother are doing now: pay for my college education with tobacco money.

There are also various organizations offering scholarships to those who have held part-time jobs during high school and those who plan to further their education. I have been able to hold a part-time job as a tobacco producer while maintaining a 3.9 grade point average, while ranking in the top 10 percent of my senior class.

There are very few students my age who have held part-time jobs and who have been able to purchase a vehicle and to pay their college expenses. Tobacco production has done this for me. What college expenses are not covered by scholarships will be solely covered by myself.

Our forefathers came to America to escape governmental restrictions and regulations. They set up a new country providing freedom of choice as outlined in our First Amendment rights.

These very rights may be taken away from the responsible tobacco consumers, but not only from the consumers, the tobacco producers may lose their rights as well.

Government could become so large that restrictions could be made on what farmers grow and how much they grow. This is big government which kills the small American citizens our very country was set up to protect.

What Causes Teen Smoking

The problem of teen smoking and smoking in general does not stem from the tobacco producer or from the tobacco companies. The problem of teen smoking lies solely with the teen's home life.

Poor family life is the core of all of society's problems. Government cannot regulate morality. This is up to each individual and/or their household. As a non-smoker, I cannot say for sure what causes teen smoking.

However, peer pressure has never been a major factor for me. Many of my friends smoke. Yet I have never felt obligated or encouraged to begin the habit. When we sit and argue over the cause of rising teen smoking rates, more and more publicity is given to this very crucial issue.

As a teenager, I can without a doubt say when adolescents hear that something is unacceptable in society, they crave the possibilities even more. Yes, teen smoking is a problem. That is not the issue.

The issue is how to curb the problem. The answer to this question lies with the family, not the government. Continuing to debate such an issue that the government should not even be considering is the greatest possible advertisement available for teen smoking.

Teen smoking must be stopped. This can be done in the home, not in Washington. Tobacco is a great part of our nation's history.

Tobacco continues to define our country for years to come. The crop provides an income of billions and provides the livelihood of thousands.

I thank you for this wonderful opportunity to testify before you today.

A BETTER WAY TO TALK TO TEENS ABOUT SMOKING

Norman E. Kjono

Norman E. Kjono is a writer and an activist for Fighting Ordinances and Restrictions to Control and Eliminate Smoking (FORCES), a smokers' rights organization. In the following essay, he discusses how he became a smoker in high school even though his parents punished him by denying him a car. As an adult who still smokes, Kjono despises tobacco opponents' attempts to eliminate smoking by demonizing smokers. Although he advises teens to choose not to smoke, he argues that teenagers must also understand that choosing to smoke does not make a person less worthy or respectable.

I returned from my first journey across the great pond to Vietnam in 1966. I was nineteen years old. One of the first things that I did was to go to the department of motor vehicles and get my driver's license.

I didn't have a driver's license or a car in high school. As I recall, that rather crimped one's social style at the time. Everyone else was out and about playing American Graffiti on Saturday night, but I had to find someone to tag along with. It was somewhat of a joke to my friends.

The reason that I didn't have a driver's license in high school was because, as my mother said, I had "muffed it" by getting caught smoking. My dad finally sold a '49 Ford that I was supposed to drive when I got my license. I guess he figured out that I wasn't going to quit smoking and gave up on having that Ford in the driveway.

I was told that if I couldn't be trusted to obey the rules at home about smoking, then I certainly couldn't be trusted to obey laws about something as important as driving a car on public roads. Besides, I was apparently committing a sin by polluting my body, which was a holy temple.

It was fine and dandy to have your holy temple dissected by 70 MM recoilless rifle or RPG incoming, by it had to be pure as the driven snow when it got blown up, I guess. Geez.

I made three more trips across the pond in various capacities with the Pacific Fleet, the last two on diesel submarines. Nice thing about

'Nam was that nobody gave you grief about the pack of Luckies that you were hauling around.

Well, life was pretty good for several years. I was honorably discharged from the US Navy in 1976 as a Chief Petty Officer after nearly thirteen years of service. I became a stock broker, then started consulting in stock and bond litigation support. I appeared on record as an expert witness in more than 150 securities fraud cases.

Then in October of 1991 a National Cancer Institute (NCI) brainstorm, the American Stop Smoking Intervention Study (Project ASSIST), was launched by Dr. Louis P. Sullivan.

Lo and behold, there stood my mother again, tapping her finger on the counter in righteous indignation about my uncivilized behavior of smoking. This time, though, they had cloned mom into thousands of activists, spread over seventeen states. I guess I just lucked out. Where I live was one of the Project ASSIST states.

This time I was not killing just myself. According to the Environmental Protection Agency (EPA) I was also killing 3,000 innocent bystanders a year. And, the clones said, I was being duped into spending good money, just to feed my *addiction*. To top it off, I was costing unspoiled folks money, to treat my diseased body.

And, to show me how bad I really was, they were going to raise the price of cigarettes with new taxes, throw me outside in the rain to smoke, and take custody of my son away from me if I consumed the evil weed in my own house.

Well, the finger tapping by anti-tobacco activists made about as much of an impression on me as mom did when I was sixteen years old. There's something about domineering activists with an axe to grind that makes me go deaf.

Lest you misunderstand, my folks are good people. They did what they thought was right, notwithstanding the fact that it didn't work, and that it was a pain in the ear to me. We get along very well nowadays, and have for years.

We declared a truce in our tobacco war by me smoking on the porch when I visit them. On the few occasions when they visit our house, I usually choose to extend them the courtesy of smoking outside. Our *family* solved our problem.

I solved the smoking problem with mom and dad in 1964 by getting out of the house. The problem with Project ASSIST, and the wellnourished pack of anti-tobacco activists that it has spawned, is that you can't get away from them. They are, quite literally, everywhere.

And it seems that everywhere you turn there's someone with a selfimage problem trying to get their ego back in balance by mandating what someone else should do. It never occurs to them that maybe just leaving people alone might be a viable option.

Which is the short version of how I got tangled up in the tobacco wars. I've been in that fire fight for several years. It's a mess. We need to find a better way, particularly for the kids.

So what do I tell my twelve-year-old son about smoking? Much the same as I tell him about other problems, like booze, drugs, and violence.

We need to start out with a simple understanding here: if Mrs. Kjono, as inspired by our local fundamentalist evangelical church, didn't stop a fifteen-year-old from smoking, then, believe me, Bill Clinton and all the professional activist "antis" combined, don't have a prayer.

To their credit, my parents were honestly trying to help me, and to guide me in a life that they thought was right. Those positive motivations are lacking with the anti-tobacco crowd. To them it's all about bucks, clout, and "mandating a difference".

So the first thing to understand is that the mandate binge displayed by the antis today didn't work with kids in the 60's, and it won't work today. It will not get the job done in the third millennium. To me, the trick is to remember how we felt as kids, then assume that our kids are pretty much the same as we were. Show a little respect for their intelligence, then give them an opportunity to make an informed choice, rather than submitting to rules. Submission is not big a priority with teenagers.

So, my good young son, here's what I have to say to you about smoking:

1. I know what I'm talking about. I've smoked for more than thirty years. No, I don't plan to quit, but that's my choice. It doesn't have to be yours.

2. I'm talking about this because I care about you, and because I am proud of the person that you have already shown yourself to be. I want the best life possible for you, and for the family that you will have one day.

3. Never do something just because someone demands that you do what they want. Likely as not, you will find that those making the loudest demands have the deepest hidden agendas. Your life is about you and those you care about, your life is not about gratifying the needs of someone with an axe to grind.

4. Part of growing up is learning how to think. You're doing a pretty good job of that so far, so let's think about a few basic realities of smoking:

    a. After you get over the dizzy hacking at first, you will find that smoking can be an enjoyable thing. I particularly enjoy a smoke with a cup of coffee after dinner, and when I get up in the morning.

    b. But the hacking that your body goes through is also telling you something. It is telling you that your body is rejecting the smoke that you inhale into your lungs. If your body instinctively rejects something, then you can bet that it probably isn't good for you. *Listen to that message from your body.*

c. The dizziness and hacking occurs because you are putting a large number of toxic contaminants into your body when you smoke. Your body will develop a tolerance for that, but why should it have to? You can avoid the physical tolerance problem by not smoking in the first place. That's a choice you can make.

d. The contaminants that you put into your physiological system by smoking have both immediate and long-term effects. You can expect that your heart, your lungs, and your circulation system will not function as well with those contaminants in your system as it will without them.

e. Over time, the negative effects of the contaminants that you put into your body by smoking tend to be cumulative. So you can expect that as you get older the effects will become more severe. You can avoid potential health problems in your later years by not starting to smoke when you are young.

f. Remember, what we do with each today determines the quality of life that we will enjoy in all of our tomorrows. Invest in your physical well-being tomorrow by taking care of your body today.

g. Since smoking imports toxic substances into your physiology, it has specific effects on your body's defense and immune systems. One of the effects is that your body consumes large quantities of natural antioxidants, such as vitamins C and E, to contend with the problems caused by smoking. That leaves less of your natural biological defenses available to handle other illnesses or diseases. Your body "using up" antioxidants can also lead to significant vitamin deficiencies, which may cause loss of hair, gum disease, loose teeth, skin rashes and other problems.

5. Considering all of the above, there are better choices for you and your health, than to start smoking. So please don't.

6. There's one more good reason why you shouldn't smoke while you're in school: it's illegal. I won't put up with you breaking laws about smoking, any more than I will accept you doing dope, beating up other kids, or stealing. You don't break those laws, so show as much respect for laws about kids smoking as you do for the other ones.

Enough said. Now, get suited up. We have soccer practice in half an hour, and as the team coach I need to be there early.

And what do I say if he starts to smoke later on, despite what I tell him? It's simple: son, I still love you. I'm still proud of you. You're still a good guy, and I still wish the best of everything for you. Remember always, your identity and self-worth do not depend on what some activist with an agenda says.

In case it wasn't clear at the beginning, neither of my parents have ever smoked. Yes, like them, I'm a good parent, too. I love and care about my boy very much.

Taxpayers just saved $368 billion.

NICOTINE: AN AUTOBIOGRAPHY

Kai Maristed

Kai Maristed, the author of the following selection, uses evoca-
tive prose to describe the experience of nicotine addiction and
withdrawal. She details how smoking often begins with adolescent experimentation and progresses into a pleasurable habit—
and an unhealthy addiction to nicotine. Quitting smoking, she
explains, is a long-term, painful process that is physically and
psychologically wrenching. Maristed is the author of the novels
Out After Dark and *Fall*.

Of all the large and small extinctions scheduled for the coming millennium, one will be mourned mainly in secret. For some, no loss is
more personal and poignant than that of the international, cos-
mopolitan solidarity of smokers. Day by day its poets and heroes,
acolytes and fellow travelers are surrendering ground to a drab two-
class society: the despised hardcore *addicts,* and the increasingly righteous majority of *nons.*

Recently, the R.J. Reynolds company launched a "no-secondhand-
smoke" cigarette, aimed at fostering the two classes' continued, if
uneasy, coexistence. In fact (according to the hoarse whispers of a
retired chemist of this butt fiend's acquaintance), a nicotine-free cigarette was perfected years ago in a Winston-Salem laboratory (the
chemist hoards a personal stash), but the project was squashed from the
top: formula patented six ways to midnight and locked away. Never
test-marketed. Whose bright idea was it to sterilize the golden goose?

You Took That First Drag Young

Drift upstream to first memories and recognize this thing in all its
transubstantiations as a kind of third parent. Mama smoked, Papa
smoked, bless the child who inhales her own. The dove-gray striations
hang in midair over playpen or crib, shiver at the transit of shadow-
bodies. Smoke trickles from adult tongues and nostrils along with the
stimulating fantastical flow of words. Older, you rise at dawn and, in
an otherwise cold and empty living room, find your parents' spoor:
butts pyramided in ashtrays, your mother's lipstick smooched onto
her brand. Traces of the absent ones. Their half-collapsed unfinished

packs prove they can't have gone far. Once, utterly absorbed, you dissect a cigarette: sample the dissolving paper and bitter-copper tobacco, peel gill by gill through the complex fibrous filter. Where does the mystery live? Years later, sobbing in adolescent desolation, you are offered a cigarette by mother or father. Sudden silence. You light up—wordless confession here—in the glow of their wistful, wondering approval. *She's nearly grown-up. Look, she's so much like us.* The point is: whatever may divide or change your mortal parents, smoking will remain their unity, your holy ghost.

In any case, you took that first drag young, so long ago that now it's difficult to recall a time when you functioned from one morning to the next with calm coordination without nicotine. That aspect of childhood seems mythical. What can it mean to "quit," when you are in significant part nicotine, just as you are made of water? But maybe in the beginning you did not light up with overt adult approval. Maybe rebellion was the goal—as you split a pack with a girlfriend, hiding out in the woods or an empty lot. To acknowledge this initiation verbally would be uncool, so instead (squinting, furiously shaking the match as it singes your thumb) you discuss rock music, or eyeliner, or French kissing. The hit creeps up inside: dizziness at first, head-sickness. You lean back against the graffiti-blasted wall. Swallow the nausea. Smile to show how you enjoy it. You *do* enjoy it; after all, you're a teenager. You are biologically and psychologically primed for contradictions: the embrace of revulsion, the seduction of risk. So this is your first time? It will be a long affair.

One in Four

Today, only one of every four adult Americans remains hooked on tobacco. Impressive decline in one generation—following the surgeon general's tirades in the late sixties—but recently the quit rate has pretty much leveled off. Now, one of us in four still huddles against the rain, or winter wind, clothes spoiling, tears in the eyes, numb frozen-sausage fingers pinching a butt. Out here, whoever we are, we don't like one another. This is not anything to have in common. Our minds flee elsewhere—back indoors to our work, or to the party, the play, or lovers' crisis continuing without us—because we don't like the selves out here. Sucking the butt. Calculating how long the fix will last. Or not last. We are one in four, the shelterless lumpen proletariat. Pollsters record that eighty percent of us *want* to quit but fail. Visitors to any hospital may notice a cordon of nurses, orderlies, and doctors, all ferociously smoking, loitering a prescribed twenty-five-foot distance from the main door.

Inhaled, dissolved in the bloodstream, nicotine strikes within eight seconds.

Nicotine, the chief alkaloid in tobacco products, binds stereoselectively to acetylcholine receptors at the autonomic ganglia, in the adrenal medulla, at neuromuscular junctions, and in the brain. Two types of central nervous system effects are . . . a stimulating effect, exerted mainly in the cortex via the locus ceruleus [which] produces increased alertness and cognitive performance. A "reward" effect via the "pleasure system" in the brain is exerted in the limbic system. At low doses the stimulant effects predominate while at high doses reward effects predominate. Intermittent intravenous administration of nicotine activates neurohormonal pathways, releasing acetylcholine, norepinephrine, dopamine, serotonin, vasopressin, beta-endorphin, growth hormone, and ACTH.

Capisce? Hard-core porn is much easier to lay hands on than serious information on nicotine, though any number of "inspirational" articles and pamphlets offer tips and tricks for controlling the "urge to light up." Do heroin users hope to get clean by sipping water, taking walks, phoning a buddy? But ex-junkies say smoking is harder to give up than dope.

The physiological information above was cribbed from an insert in the patch kit (prescription only, $25), a microscopic text addressed to medical doctors. (The box also contains a how-to in large print for the lay user.) To the butt fiend, this grim sketch of the "pleasure system" foreshadows even more ominous implications. So nicotine transforms to—or replaces—acetylcholine? Consider: as you have smoked with hardly a break since early adolescence, won't your body have lost all ability to make the natural chemical? A form of atrophy? Is the loss reversible? If so, after how long? Meanwhile, what happens in the brain without acetylcholine: raw nerves rasping like metal on metal, without the emollients of serotonin, dopamine, and the rest? Slippage of concentration? Mental seize-up? Or is all this just an excuse, are you exaggerating, paranoid, inventing agonies to come?

Another snip: the *New York Times* (August 31, 1994) reports that "some people's genes may predispose them to both smoking and depression." Psychiatrists suggest these unfortunates choose between nicotine or Prozac. This is a choice? For some doomed quitters, even Prozac brings no relief, and "smoking may be the lesser of two evils, since life is not worth living under the constant drain of depression." There is active suicide, and there is passive suicide, and sometimes fear feels like nothing more than hyperactive depression.

You and Lauren Bacall

So why not switch to gum or the patch? No stain, no smell, no sticky carcinogenic compounds. The drug pure and simple, in a sanitary, socially sanctioned delivery form. It would be like going on methadone. Why not?

OVERDOSAGE: The oral minimum acute lethal dose in human adults is 40 to 60 mg (less than 1 mg per kilo). . . . Symptoms of poisoning include pallor, cold sweat, nausea, vomiting, abdominal pain, disturbed hearing and vision, peripheral paralysis.

It's not just the tar, stupid. Or the two-hundred-odd additives. It's a unique compound, $C_{10}H_{14}N_2$, this central soothing and stimulating miracle molecule, nicotine.

According to Lauren Bacall (who, despite Bogie's fatal cancer, went on smoking), the stagey business with cigarettes is thoroughly and boldly erotic, a semiotic of seduction in real life as on the screen. Wordless intimacy, often between strangers: widened eyes reflecting the shared flame, fingertips brushing. The hazy expulsion of pleasure, through relaxed, parted lips.

You hate propaganda. You despise the self-appointed smoke militia, with its Frankenstein's-lung horror posters and public humiliation tactics. To quintuple the cigarette tax showed majority rule in action (since three out of four voters won't pay), but none of the windfall goes to redeem the sinners from their vice. Meanwhile, strangers stop you on the street to say you are killing your children. Presumably these are the same vigilant citizens who want to jail pregnant women for drinking alcohol. These days, puffing in public feels daring again: a political act.

Even in pregnancy, you never exactly quit—although morning sickness imposed limits. Later—while smoking—you anxiously observed each baby for telltale stuntedness. As for your own mother, she smoked on with gusto and abandon until the tracheotomy in her cancerous throat forced a sudden no-backsliding policy. Watching her waste away, you did not dream of quitting. On the contrary. It was a stressful time, and without snatched respites of inflating your lungs with a cloud—then rising on its wave of nicotine—you'd have lost your grip completely. Hey, baby: you and Lauren Bacall.

Tobacco's Pleasures

Two or three packs a day. But no cough, no symptoms, heaven knows weight's no problem, and you're healthier than most your age. The smoke curling from under your study door is a family joke. Work hard: the price per pack keeps ratcheting up. At least you don't squander money on frills.

At a party someone asks: Why can't we use tobacco the way the Indians did? Once a month or so the tribe gathered, old and young, men and women, they passed the pipe, got buzzed, had some visions—then they could leave it alone. Why can't we?

Ah, the mouthwatering cigarettes of Europe. The aromas of steeped espresso and black tobacco tangle in sidewalk cafes. Schoolgirls with round creamy faces chain-smoke cigarettes, as do drop-dead elegant old women. Here's freedom. Here's to the republic of enlightened pleasure. (You wake up in your hotel room in the dark before dawn, clammy from the recurrent inexplicable nightmare of dying by your own hand. Switch on the lamp, fumble for a Gitane filter, with fingers stained ocher yellow.)

Quitting

One year later, in Boston, a receptionist collects our checks. Sixty dollars times twenty-five "clients": no shabby wage for two hours of wonder-curing. Sultry summer afternoon. Climate of last-ditch hope and boisterous confession: we trump each other's stories, laughing in the relief of self-abasement. The famous healer enters. He is short with a trim beard and has preserved his furry Russian accent. We strain to identify words. While pacing inside our circle, talking, talking, he insists he is not a hypnotist. Stare at any man long enough and you will either fall in love or in hate. He pounces on the miracle—for one whole hour no one here has smoked. As the finale, we each receive a moment of personal concentration. He splays pale manicured hands over my head and sighs, "You have beautiful body. Must take care for it, please." Please.

Outside I feel uplifted—or already woozy from withdrawal. This determination to not-smoke is like biting down on a coin while undergoing an unpleasant medical procedure. Determination lasts all the way to the middle of the next morning. When it collapses, the first almost-virginal, mind-bending, releasing drag tastes alien, like a swig of lifesaving water from a dirty, rusted pipe.

Your youngest child would rather sing and dance than plug into Nintendo. But this winter he's tortured by a series of colds and coughs. Bruise-brown smudges appear under his eyes. One day, audible in his breath is a faint fogged whistle in each inhalation, like wind soughing at the end of a long cave. Does he notice this sound himself? Oh, he says, it's nothing special. For a long time now, he can't breathe in all the way.

Not-smoking hurts. You picture your brain as remodeled by Oz: all cotton wool and flashing needles. After an hour, two at most, an intense constriction radiates from your chest—the heart—outward through shoulders and arms and down through the lobes of lungs. Paradoxically, not-smoking unleashes this sense of acute suffocation.

What is not true: that chewing on pencils, jellybeans, or any placebo can dull the edge of this claustrophobic tension; nor can fingering worry beads, or knitting, or sipping all-day liquids. So it's not oral satisfaction, or toys to fiddle with, that you crave. The truth is: as your nicotine titer drops, the neural network is being frayed and flayed apart. Nerves scream for the chemical they need to reconnect.

Also not true: that you are excessively irritable or uncontrolled. On the contrary, every not-smoking moment is a monument to extreme self-control. (In your worst dream, you notice an already half-smoked cigarette wedged between your fingers.) You may even be more tolerant of others than before. An inner catastrophe puts minor disturbances in perspective.

As after any devastating breakup, along with weeping jags, guilt spasms, resurgent desire, sleeplessness, apathy, incredulity, and the rest, comes virulent hatred. My nose is morbidly sensitive. I won't enter rooms that hold a recollection of smoke. To see someone light up gives me a queasy rush, like watching a surgeon's incision. I hate the tobacco companies and how their genius for exploitation exemplifies the sanctioned cannibalism of our species. As a girl, I used to see myself mirrored in the magazine ads for Parliaments and Winstons—prophetically prettier, adept at tennis or sailing, bookended by adoring males. With each cigarette I consumed, the infinite distance between myself and that image felt halved.

Times change. The market strategists' targets for the year 2000 in the United States are small kids. Poor city kids: the Little Friends of Joe Camel. But will there be enough budding butt fiends to save Joe? Not to worry. The serious money will come from smoke in distant places. Ad campaigns in Asia and Africa already depict female smokers as educated, affluent progressives, making a successful raid on the traditional bag of male privilege. There's truth to this, of course. And imagine: out there swarm billions of potential new customers. Girls discarding the veil, entering the factory, savoring that heady, hard-earned first drag. It's exciting. There's still a killing to be made in tobacco stocks.

You Are Not Yourself

What seemed unutterably necessary is gone. What was always knotted so tightly into minutes and hours has been stripped out. The days lurch along without punctuation. How to end a meal? Complete a phrase? Launch into a phone call? Blunt boredom, stifle hunger, anesthetize the heart against an insult or a break?

Who on earth are you now, anyway?

Paradoxically, this pervasive dizziness, this goofy light-headedness is a lot like those powerful first smokes. The short-term memory is shot to hell, though. Names mean nothing, calls go unreturned, plans are jettisoned, deadlines blown. Time seems both compressed and elongated, squeezed like a gummi-worm. But someone still wakes, sleeps, cries, and laughs, too. Apparently some kind of you is continuing without the old central assumption, deep-sigh rhythm of inspiration. Just how flimsy are the rest of the assumptions that make up "you"?

Would you suffer for any principle? What are your other addictions? Are you an alcoholic, salt or caffeine abuser, raving egotist, love junkie? Do you love those whom you say you love? Aren't the attributes you claim—"shy," "ambitious," "loyal," for example—merely

chance conventions? You are in fact bold, complacent, and faithless.
Is there anyone who could know you?
We hear you're quitting. We understand that you are not yourself.
No, but facing a choice between suicide and loss of marbles, it seems better to go crazy. At least you can still change your mind.
You must be proud of yourself! they say.
A. Alvarez, from his recent book *Night:*

> Loewi prepared two frogs, stimulated the vagus nerve of one, causing its heartbeat to slow down, then transferred the blood from the first frog's heart to the second's; when that slowed too, Loewi had his answer: nerves . . . transmitted their signals chemically. Later it was shown that the chemical in question, Loewi's *vagustoff* was acetylcholine, the neuro-transmitter that triggers dreams.

You sleep as if clubbed, but for only a few hours at a time. Instead of dreams you have waking hyperreal hallucinations. Daily, you weep. This is all chemical, don't forget. No sense looking for a "cause" for your constant anxiety, although certain randomly fired images—of a snowy street in Berlin, for example, of a stray cat purring over milk, of a sick friend outlined by the light of a window—can twist the anxiety to a new pitch. All of these images show something that no longer exists. They are about loss.

Fairy-Tale Rewards

As in a fairy tale, rewards for the done deed materialize out of nowhere. Amazing—for once in life, promises are kept. Revisit that mirror: now that Cinderella has quit playing with ashes, her eyes are clear, her teeth pearlier, her cheeks rosy from a fresh supply of hemo-globin. Open the medicine cabinet, toss out aspirin, tablets and syrups against nausea and heartburn. You haven't needed any of this in weeks.

The newly laid-on five pounds of flesh make it easier to sit on hard chairs as well as to stay outdoors in winter. Even in freezing weather there's a reassuring sting of circulation in fingers and toes. Improved circulation brings other awarenesses and awakenings. From butt fiend to sex fiend—is that the happy ending?

You sprint across parking lots, dash two-steps-at-a-time up stairs. Often one of these exuberant bursts releases a second level of power and stamina. You might as well be flying. Physical energy demands outlet—you scrub the smoke-yellowed windows and walls, vacuum exuberantly. Cinderella, who used to suffer embarrassment over so many things—her dull gray skin, russet fingers, the smell of the house to visitors—now shudders at the whiff from a smoker's smile. That stench of decay. *Get away, Death-Breath!* Now, rooms which used to hold pots of ashes offer bowls of dried perfumed flowers instead. You can take a walking tour of good smells. Hey, Cinderella, high on all these changes—admit that your house has never before been nearly so nice and clean. . . .

Missing Nicotine

Incredible. So you've actually done it, friends say.

Nothing's "done" yet. The friends tend to lower their voices on the subject of smoking, as if afraid of starting off the avalanche of my backslide. Understandable. Statistically, women who have smoked since trainer-bra days don't stand much chance. I know a sports pro who cold turkeyed for five months, then, laughing like a lunatic at her defeat, caved in. I know a quadruple bypass survivor who mail orders gourmet cigars. There's a drugstore clerk here, smokeless ten years, who bitches about her unabated craving with every pack she sells.

I'm lonely. I've joined a health club, pay to jog on a treadmill, and don't even smile at the joke. Evenings I don't pretend to work. I'm hotly envious of the stars in TV movies—how they can smoke in the role, with the grand gesture. At the apex of terror or joy, the stars raise half-closed eyes to heaven and suck in the miasma, as if re-inhaling their own souls. Suddenly I remember what it was like to have heart's balm literally at one's fingertips.

It's been five months. I don't miss the taste or ritual, but who can tell me whether I'll ever find a way back to myself—to simply being instead of changing. Back to being me. Able to work as I used to, to concentrate, to grapple with a concept. Here, this is the hardest temptation: missing nicotine as soul food, to fill the void where I used to be.

I go looking for the past and by luck rediscover a friend who disappeared more than ten years ago. When we were young and outrageous, we danced together in disco contests, dated two brothers, praised each other, shared favorite clothes and shelter. I'm glad to have found her again.

These days she lives in a penthouse, an uncurtained fishbowl in the clouds. Her parents have passed away. She beat alcoholism by throwing her whiskey in the river two years ago. She was a good architect but no longer needs to work. There's no furniture. My friend sits on the floor, which is a sea bottom of possessions—books, pottery, unhung paintings, shoes, unwashed dishes—all dusty, filmed with ash or oil. With her strong hands and sure movements (she once apprenticed to a carpenter), she is rolling a homemade cigarette. Giving a sideways grin, she holds up fingers briefly to show that they no longer tremble. Her fingers are yellow, her teeth are brown. It's hard for me to look at her etched frown and wrinkle-puckered lips. Carefully, she pokes a few crumbs of hashish, recently legalized where she lives, into the tobacco threads.

"Don't lecture, okay?"

"I know it's useless. I won't."

"The dope," she says, "I think I could give up. I've done it before. But nicotine is something else."

Two days later, she drives me to the station. Smoking a fat one down to the last gram. Flicking that scrap away, down into the track, so we can hug good-bye. We're both crying. Her tears slide through my hair. Her low voice resonates in my own head. "The only thing that might give me the strength for it," she says, "is if you ask me to quit because you love me."

"Please. I love you!"

Then I climb on the train and find a window to watch her walk away.

At home sometimes, in an apprehensive reflex, I still hold my breath and listen. But the frightening sounds are gone. My little boy's chest is clear, he doesn't gasp or cough, no matter how recklessly he sings.

CHAPTER 4

REDUCING AND
PREVENTING TEEN
SMOKING

Contemporary Issues
Companion

Authorities Seek Out the Right Antismoking Message for Teenagers

John Schwartz

Adolescent rebelliousness makes it difficult to gauge the success of antismoking programs for youths, reports *Washington Post* staff writer John Schwartz. He writes that some tobacco education efforts have seemingly backfired, as was the case in Arizona, where many teens acquired antitobacco T-shirts simply to be seen smoking while wearing them. On the other hand, Schwartz points out, strongly enforced restrictions on youth access to cigarettes and tobacco promotional products in retail stores can be effective ways to reduce teen smoking. Many researchers maintain that the designers of youth antismoking programs must continually adjust their strategies until they discover what works, Schwartz concludes.

When the state of Arizona launched a multimillion-dollar anti-smoking campaign, officials decided to target youths by appealing to them in their own language. The slogan "Tobacco. Tumor causing, teeth staining, smelly puking habit," became nearly ubiquitous beginning in 1996, emblazoned on T-shirts, billboards, caps, pens, key chains, boxer shorts and more across the state.

It was the most visible part of a $30-million tobacco education and cessation program. It was tough. It was in your face. And with some kids, at least, it backfired.

Just ask 16-year-old Ashley Lane, whose friends donned the T-shirts so they could be seen wearing them while smoking. Some even burned cigarette holes in the shirts. "We all thought it was a joke, basically. . . . Like 'Look at me, ha ha,' outright defiance. It was like, 'Yeah, right, whatever.'"

Mixed Results on Anti-Tobacco Campaigns

As Congress considers legislation to implement a national tobacco settlement aimed at cutting youth smoking, Arizona's experience

illustrates a sobering fact: No one really knows what works. [A comprehensive federal anti-smoking bill failed in June 1998. However, in
a November 1998 civil settlement, the tobacco industry agreed to pay
46 states $206 billion and to submit to advertising and marketing
restrictions.]

State and local campaigns in this country and others have tried
many approaches to stop children from smoking, including price
increases, crackdowns on sales to minors, and restrictions on advertising and promotional activities that appeal to young people. The
efforts have produced promising, but decidedly mixed, results.

"We have made some fundamental assumptions, and they're based
on our intuitive grasp—but they are not based on hard fact," says
Richard Clayton, head of a cessation-research program at the University of Kentucky. "The science is emerging on this but it hasn't in any
strong sense arrived."

Tobacco control experts say that little has been done to effectively
gauge the success of youth programs, and that science appears to be
far from determining how to overcome what is perhaps the most per-
plexing obstacle: the contrariness of the adolescent mind.

"The truth is we really don't know a lot about what we can do,"
says John Pierce of the University of California at San Diego, who
measures smoking behavior for the state. "We certainly know that
we're getting blown away by the industry at the moment."

Increasing Acceptance of Smoking

Despite all of the anti-tobacco efforts in recent years, teenagers' attitudes toward smoking are growing more positive. Since 1991, the pro-
portion of eighth-graders who say they disapprove of smoking a pack
a day has fallen from 83 percent to 77 percent; among 12th-graders,
from 71 percent to 67 percent, according to the University of Michigan's nationwide "Monitoring the Future" survey.

Today, about 90 percent of smokers take up the habit before they
turn 18, public health officials say; 3,000 kids try smoking each day,
and an estimated 1,000 become regular smokers. In 1996, 30 percent
of 10th-graders and 34 percent of 12th-graders had smoked in the previous month, and smoking jumped by nearly half among eighth- and
10th-graders between 1991 and 1996.

But research on exactly what factors lead young people to smoke is
murky. They appear to be a blend of parental smoking, peer pressure
and advertising, says Richard Pollay, a tobacco advertising expert at
the University of British Columbia. "Any reasonable judgment shows
that there is an influential role of advertising. It's impossible to quan-
tify exactly its contribution relative to other factors like peer pressure—but it contributes to these other factors."

Ashley Lane started smoking in 1995. "It wasn't like people were
passing a cigarette and I said 'Well, okay, I guess.' I went to look for

who could give me cigarettes so I could go smoking. I
be part of the party crowd and that was part of it." She
........ner first smokes off of a couple of worldly 11-year-olds.

Ashley had been an honor student and athlete, but like many teen-agers hit emotional shoals in middle school. "I was fighting with my parents a lot and I was getting real depressed." She said that she read youth magazines warning that adolescents who get depressed often turn to tobacco for solace—and took it as a prescription. "I said, 'Really? If that's what people in my situation do, why shouldn't I do it?'"

Youths Often Underestimate Tobacco's Dangers

Many youngsters, studies show, don't understand the extent of tobacco's health risks, with only 50 percent of eighth-graders saying that a pack-a-day smoker runs a great risk of harm; 68 percent of 12th-graders reported that level of risk. They also don't see the extent of tobacco's addictiveness, research has shown. Between 1975 and 1985, approximately 75 percent of people who had smoked daily during high school were still daily smokers from seven to nine years later; only 5 percent of them had predicted in high school, however, that they would still be smoking at that time, according to figures cited by the Centers for Disease Control and Prevention.

Still, many young smokers are well aware of the risks—and, in fact, are among the brightest teenagers.

"I knew what I was doing was stupid," Lane says, "but I wanted to do it anyway."

Likewise, Simone, a Montgomery County high school student who requested anonymity because she does not want her parents to know she smokes as many as a half-dozen cigarettes daily, says knowing the risks doesn't deter her, or her friends, because "A lot of kids have this immortality thing going," she explains. "They think they're invincible."

An honor student, Simone has heard all the talk about the influences on teenagers—peer pressure, advertising and more—but "It wasn't anyone telling me to try it. It was me saying, 'Why not?'"

Simone said she smokes for the same reason many adults do: to ease the stress of daily life. Tenth grade is tough, she says, and smoking "gives me five or 10 minutes to think about something besides homework and besides deadlines and projects and teachers."

Anti-Smoking Efforts

A number of local anti-smoking programs have produced some results. Woodridge, Ill., imposed tough restrictions on young people's access to tobacco products, and spot checks to make sure stores aren't selling to kids. That program has been credited with bringing smoking rates down by 50 percent among the town's 12- to 14-year-olds. And when 24 California cities and towns adopted local ordinances prohibiting self-service merchandising and tobacco promotional products in retail stores, estimated tobacco sales to minors dropped by 40 percent to 80 percent.

But a recent study of several local anti-tobacco programs in Massachusetts showed that unless at least 90 percent of stores comply with tobacco age laws, they don't work—because teenagers soon find the scofflaw stores and buy to their hearts' content. "It's almost like a speakeasy," says Nancy Rigotti, director of tobacco research and treatment at Boston's Massachusetts General hospital and Harvard Medical School.

In recent years, tobacco control experts have rallied around stiff price increases as an effective weapon. President Bill Clinton embraced this idea in September 1997 when he called for per-pack cigarette prices to rise by as much as $1.50 over the next 10 years if targets for reducing underage smoking aren't met. The evidence for this theory is encouraging, but also far from conclusive.

Frank J. Chaloupka, an economist at the University of Illinois-Chicago, says his research indicates that youngsters are three times as sensitive to price increases as adults. Chaloupka analyzed statistics from the University of Michigan's survey and estimates that a 10 percent increase in cigarette prices triggers a 13 percent reduction in cigarette consumption by teenagers overall and a nearly 7 percent reduction in the numbers of teenagers who smoke.

Canada raised taxes on tobacco products rapidly, from 42 Canadian cents in 1984 to $1.93 in 1992. Youth smoking rates fell by an estimated 60 percent. But black market activity increased as well along the U.S. border, and under pressure from the tobacco industry, the government lowered tobacco taxes. "Smoking rates among kids also began to rise for the first time in a decade," said Matthew L. Myers of the National Center for Tobacco-Free Kids.

Tobacco companies, however, have argued that stiff price increases will do more harm than good. Jay Martin, chief operating officer of the National Tobacco Co., says the price increases would promote black markets and by driving adults out of the market would hurt entire industries that depend on tobacco sales—not just companies like his, but also the network of wholesalers and the convenience stores and candy stores they serve.

Worse, he argues, the programs will not budge youth smoking rates. "They're going to get the product if they want to get it," Martin says. "If these kids are spending a hundred bucks for a pair of tennis shoes, you think three bucks or four bucks for a pack of cigarettes is going to bother them?" Younger smokers, after all, select the most-heavily advertised brands—Marlboro and Camel—which tend to be the most expensive. And youth smoking rates have remained stubbornly high in Britain and Scandinavia despite hefty tobacco prices, Martin notes.

Tobacco control advocates agree that some young people will continue to smoke no matter what, which is why most programs aim at reducing teenage smoking, not eliminating it. "As long as they see it as something that's cool and carries all kinds of social and psychological benefits that are portrayed in movies and advertising and the media in general, some kids will be able to afford it," says Lloyd D. Johnston, who heads the Michigan study.

A Combination of Tools

Thus tobacco control experts have concluded that it takes a combination of tools—including school-based programs, restrictions on access and advertising as well as price increases—to fight underage tobacco use. "The one thing we know is there is no single magic bullet," Myers says. "Only a comprehensive plan has any chance of success over the long run."

The Clinton administration has gradually broadened its approach to include over time, access restriction, advertising bans and most recently price increases.

This gradual shift in strategy angers the tobacco industry and its allies. Democratic Sen. Wendell H. Ford of Kentucky has noted that some of the same officials who pledged in 1996 that a Food and Drug Administration plan would reduce youth smoking by 50 percent in seven years have since argued that similar provisions of the proposed national tobacco settlement cannot work without the price increase. Tobacco industry officials suggest that ever-tougher proposals raise questions about the true motives of anti-tobacco activists.

"I just find it fascinating how the goalposts were moved," complains an attorney for the tobacco industry. "All the old things that used to be panaceas are no longer meaningful. . . . Doesn't it make you wonder if the true goal isn't to do as much damage to the industry as possible?"

One prominent anti-smoking researcher says that the focus on underage smokers is fundamentally flawed. Because of the importance of adults as role models, "It is impossible to reduce teen smoking in a vacuum," says Stanton Glantz of the University of California at San Francisco. "When teens see adults rejecting tobacco and tobacco use, they will," Glantz says.

For example, the first few years that California commissioned ads beginning in 1989, the campaigns were directed against tobacco use across the board. Adult smoking dropped at the height of the first campaign, and underage smoking held steady while rising elsewhere in the United States. Since then, the state has refocused its campaigns on teenage smoking, and rates there have begun to rise once more, Glantz says.

New programs are trying to come up with solid ways to measure the effectiveness of youth smoking programs. In Tucson, the Robert

Wood Johnson Foundation is spending more than $3 million on a program called Full Court Press that uses teenagers to reach their peers directly. Unlike Arizona's state program, which never mentions the role of the tobacco industry, Full Court Press's teenage representatives speak harshly of tobacco industry "lies" and youth-oriented advertising.

"When they learn adults and industry are targeting them with campaigns and laughing all the way to the bank, it touches a personal chord with them," says Donna Grande, director of the program. Just as important, Grande says, the foundation has allocated nearly a million dollars more to determine the effectiveness of the Tucson efforts over five years.

Ultimately, any approach that tries to second-guess the teenage psyche might backfire. As author Richard Kluger warns in his history of the tobacco history, *Ashes to Ashes,* many teenagers smoke "not in spite of the hazards associated with it but because of them." The tobacco industry appears to understand this. A 1973 memorandum from R.J. Reynolds Tobacco Co. examined youth smoking issues and observed that "if the 'older' establishment is preaching against smoking, the anti-establishment sentiment discussed above would cause the young to want to be defiant and smoke."

Rigotti, who conducted the study showing that many youth access programs aren't effective, says: "Some people could read the study and say 'it's not working, let's stop bothering to try.'. . . My answer to that is 'Just because your first pass at a solution doesn't work doesn't mean you give up. You keep adjusting your tactics until you find what works.'"

PUTTING OUT THE FLAME OF DESIRE

S.J. Diamond

Criminalizing underage smoking may help curb tobacco use among teens, argues S.J. Diamond in the following selection. Diamond notes that some people might question the wisdom of implementing antismoking laws in the midst of seemingly more serious youth problems such as drug abuse and gang violence. However, the author points out, the enforcement of youth smoking laws—which typically require teens to pay fines and attend corrective classes—will make youngsters think twice about smoking. Diamond is a resident of Los Angeles, California.

Talking and smoking, my 17-year-old son and a friend stood outside the old Fox Theater in Westwood, California, before the show. Up came a policeman, asked for their driver's licenses and said they were smoking illegally. Then, after searching them, he gave them citations ordering them to appear at Juvenile Court on a 308(b) penal code violation: possession of tobacco by a minor.

They were shocked, and worried about losing their licenses, if not their freedom. As their parents, we were equally shocked, but ambivalent. With everything going on nowadays—drugs, gangs, robberies—this didn't seem the best use of police or court time. But the smoking was an ongoing battle, and we welcomed whatever help the village would provide in raising our children.

Criminalizing Underage Smoking

Actually, the village's commitment isn't clear-cut. It was California's grocers who helped toughen the law, which originally made it a crime for minors to buy or receive tobacco products. Selling to minors was also illegal, with stiffer penalties, and grocers were tired of youngsters coming in—or being sent in by anti-smoking advocates—and going from checker to checker until someone slipped up.

"There's a shared responsibility here," said California Grocers Assn. President Peter Larkin. "If we expect to eliminate smoking in minors, everyone has a role, including the minor."

At the behest of the grocers' association, the Legislature passed a bill that took effect in January 1997, making the act of underage smoking a crime.

To those enforcing the law—Los Angeles police, sheriff's deputies, school police—teenage smoking isn't a big concern. It's important only in association with other behaviors that come under the Juvenile Court citation program—loitering, violating curfew, alcohol abuse and drug possession. Because youngsters in groups are often smoking, an officer can walk up and cite them for that while looking for other problems.

The Los Angeles Police Department alone handed out 900 smoking citations in 1997, and each of the county's 10 Juvenile Courts are handling up to 100 a month.

For a youth who has never been to court, that's where the smoking ticket gets serious.

Dressed, combed and accompanied by parents, my son and his friend checked in at Juvenile Court in Santa Monica, took numbers, found seats in the crowd and obeyed the sign saying "Quiet. Court in Session." They read and signed a statement of their rights.

Finally, each in turn was called before the Juvenile Court referee— high bench, black robe and all. He lectured them briefly about smoking and issued the kicker: There's a "mandatory minimum fine of $246"—actually a fine of $75, plus a penalty of $17 for each $10 of fine, plus $35 for late payment. But attending an eight-hour smoking program could reduce it—to $35 for the Corrective Behavior Institute, which puts on the program, and $35 for the court.

The Corrective Behavior Institute

In court, smoking isn't treated as secondary to anything. It's "a gateway drug," said Long Beach Juvenile Court Referee Claire Vermillion, "because smoking is a risk-taking behavior."

The same point was made to the two teenagers at their smoking seminar, one of several Corrective Behavior Institute programs to which courts now refer youths cited for drinking, drug use, traffic violations, truancy, shoplifting and "reckless behavior."

Held at a church, the seminar was a standard stop-smoking program.

But these were kids, and cool. Most were boys, many only 13 or 14, who had been ticketed by school police. A few were tossed out of the seminar for foul language. Some were already beyond tobacco.

"They were like, 'Hey, I was dealing coke on the corner when the cops come by, give me a ticket for dealing and a ticket for smoking as well,'" my son said.

To teenagers, the mortality issue is, in my son's words, "just b.s." But some kids, he says, "will think it over because it's a pain in the tail to go to court and to these classes."

Whatever. Any pain will serve, even the pain of boredom.

"It's important to hold the kids accountable," said Pamela A. Davis, Juvenile Court referee in Santa Monica, "so they see there are consequences, that it's going to be a hassle. The harder it is, the less enjoyable it'll be to smoke."

The smoking cases are dealt with quickly. But even if they become a hassle, it will be worth it—for teenage smokers and the rest of the village as well.

EARLY CHILDHOOD NURTURING WOULD CURB TEEN SMOKING

T. Berry Brazelton

T. Berry Brazelton argues that an emphasis on high-quality child care—particularly in the first three years of life—will lead to a reduction in teen smoking. Early nurturing helps the brain develop, he writes, and fosters a healthy self-image and a strong motivation for learning among children. Emotionally healthy children are less likely to take up smoking, Brazelton maintains. Low-income working families should therefore be given the financial support they need to pay for quality child care, he concludes. Brazelton is professor emeritus of pediatrics at Harvard Medical School and the author of several books on child-rearing. When this selection was written, the U.S. Senate was debating a federal antismoking bill, the main goal of which was to reduce teenage smoking. This bill failed in June 1998; however, as of March 1999, future federal antitobacco legislation was pending.

The Senate began debate in May 1998 on bipartisan tobacco legislation, and both Republicans and Democrats agree that the number one goal of this bill is to reduce teenage smoking. Rightfully so. After all, millions of young lives hang in the balance. [This federal antismoking bill did not pass.]

There has already been much discussion about restricting tobacco advertising and increasing the price of cigarettes to curb teen smoking. But before the debate is over, Congress should consider the underlying realities that make children vulnerable to the lure of tobacco—and invest some of the resources in the essential early-childhood development and care that can really help us save children from the dangers of smoking.

The Need for Early Nurturing

This investment in child development is a smart public health strategy based on sound science.

Recent research reminds us of the crucial importance of the first three years of life. It is during these early years that the vast majority

Reprinted, with permission, from "To Curb Teen Smoking, Nurture Children in Their Earliest Years," by T. Berry Brazelton, *Boston Globe*, May 21, 1998.

of brain growth and development occurs. And by shaping the structure of a baby's brain, these early experiences begin to shape the baby's self image, capacity for altruism, and motivation for learning.

Television and news magazines have carried pictures of the brains of two young children growing up with very different experiences. These pictures are road maps to our nation's future. One picture is of a healthy brain, showing how appropriate early nurturing "wires the circuits" for success. The other picture is of a far less healthy brain, showing the missed connections and lost opportunities resulting from lack of needed early stimulation.

In many ways, this "wiring" of the brain creates the solid foundation on which a child's ability to learn, solve problems, and eventually succeed is carefully constructed. If we wait until adolescence to help our children develop the sense of self that is needed to resist the draw of smoking, we will be sorry.

If we want the best for our children, if we want their earliest years to lay the groundwork for a bright and smoke-free future, we must ensure that they receive the nurturing and stimulation they need from the start.

Young children's experiences with early learning help shape the way they feel, think, learn, and behave for the rest of their lives. High-quality child care can help our youngest children enter school ready to learn and develop the life skills they will need to steer clear of unhealthy habits such as smoking, drinking, and drug use.

Every day in America, millions of low-income families face the daunting task of paying for quality child care on limited budgets. This is today's reality for families who have no choice but to work, a reality that leaves far too many children at risk. Low-income parents need support to ensure that their children are safe and well cared for during these formative years. Unfortunately, far too few of them receive the help they need and deserve.

Quality Child Care as a Strategy

The research is conclusive—early investments have a lifelong impact. And the payoff is healthier children. But research alone will not reduce teen smoking or build healthy futures. This requires action. Congress should remember the research and help us to move this knowledge from paper to practice. Here's how.

Congress should pass strong and bipartisan tobacco legislation that recognizes the important connection between early learning and reducing teen smoking. And it should invest tobacco tax money in expanding access and improving the quality of child care. Setting aside a portion of the more than $500 billion generated by this potential legislation would make an enormous difference for millions of children.

The Commerce Committee wisely included child care and after-school activities among the priority areas for investment of tobacco revenue. The president did the same in his budget proposal. The full Senate should now pass the Kerry-Bond amendment to make that promise a reality. [This amendment to the failed 1998 tobacco settlement bill would have earmarked a portion of tobacco tax revenues to fund child-care programs.]

If we want our children to be smart enough to say no to tobacco, then Congress needs to be smart enough to say yes to making child care and after-school programs part of our national strategy for keeping kids healthy and tobacco-free. As a prescription for preventing teen smoking, these programs are just what the doctor ordered.

BEWARE OF THE TOBACCO INDUSTRY'S "PREVENTION" PROGRAMS

Americans for Nonsmokers' Rights

Americans for Nonsmokers' Rights (ANR) is an antismoking advocacy organization based in Berkeley, California. In the following selection, ANR examines several antismoking programs for youth that are backed by the tobacco industry. These programs include several plans for restricting youth access to tobacco, educational agendas that emphasize smoking as an adult activity, and support for policies that punish teens for possessing cigarettes. Such programs, ANR contends, actually make cigarettes more attractive to teens by emphasizing tobacco as a "forbidden fruit" and smoking as a choice that "only adults" can make. By supporting these programs, the organization asserts, the tobacco industry manages to boost its public image while subtly advertising its product to teenagers. ANR urges those concerned about youth smoking to steer away from any antismoking programs supported by the tobacco industry.

One of the most visible and hypocritical strategies of the tobacco industry is the development of its own educational programs. These programs fall loosely into two categories: youth access programs and educational programs. The most disturbing aspect of these programs is that many businesses and individuals have fallen for the tobacco industry's ruse. Two examples include Danny Glover's representation of R.J. Reynolds on behalf of its "Support The Law—It Works" program and the tobacco companies' JAYS (Jaycees Against Youth Smoking) program.

There is, however, an important instructive value to the tobacco industry's own "anti-tobacco" programs. We have long relied on the tobacco industry's own reactions to anti-tobacco strategies as a means of assessing our own effectiveness. In other words, if the tobacco industry adopts a given strategy, then that strategy is probably ineffective at controlling tobacco use (or may even backfire). Conversely,

Reprinted, with permission, from "Tobacco Industry 'Prevention' Programs," an online report by Americans for Nonsmokers' Rights, published September 1998 at www. no-smoke.org/ind_prog.html.

if the tobacco industry aggressively opposes an anti-tobacco effort, we have evidence that that particular strategy is effective.

Tobacco Industry Youth Access Programs

• *"It's the Law."* This was the Tobacco Institute's first major "youth access" program, now retired. The primary component of "It's the Law" was the distribution of blue signs with white and orange lettering which read: "It's the Law: We Do Not Sell Tobacco Products to Persons Under 18." In late 1990, the Tobacco Institute announced a $10 million public relations campaign surrounding "It's the Law." In addition to posting signs, the program also included:

  • Support for legislation requiring supervision of tobacco vending machines.
  • Voluntary restrictions on tobacco billboard placement and free sampling of tobacco products.
  • Distribution of the Tobacco Institute/C.O.U.R.S.E. Consortium booklet, "Helping Youth Say No".

Not surprisingly, a 1996 article published in the *American Journal of Public Health* found "It's the Law" programs were not associated with a significant reduction in illegal sales either with vending machines or over-the-counter sources. Tobacco control activists long suspected that the actual purpose of the program was to improve the low public image of the tobacco industry, while legitimizing certain industry lobbying efforts. With the forced release of internal industry documents, this suspicion has been confirmed.

• *"Support The Law—It Works."* Much like "It's the Law," this was R.J. Reynolds' first "comprehensive" retail program. The program was most notable for having enlisted actor Danny Glover as its spokesperson. "Support The Law—It Works" bore many similarities to the Tobacco Institute's "It's the Law," including a focus on signage and on framing smoking as an adult activity.

• *"We Card."* In 1995, amidst great fanfare, the Coalition for Responsible Tobacco Retailing, whose members included cigarette and smokeless tobacco companies and leading convenience store and supermarket chains, unveiled a new national voluntary program to combat tobacco sales to minors. The program, heavily backed by the Tobacco Institute, centers on having store clerks ask for picture identification from anyone appearing younger than 25 before selling them any tobacco product. Participating stores receive signs that read, "Under 18. We Card. No Tobacco," together with employee training guides, a calendar indicating the date of birth required to legally purchase tobacco, and various pins, pads, and decals. Substantively, the program is quite similar to the "It's the Law" program, which it replaced.

• *"Action Against Access."* Philip Morris (PM) is touting their latest program, Action Against Access (AAA), as one of the most comprehensive programs ever introduced to combat youth access to cigarettes. Designed as a complement to the "We Card" program, AAA purports to discourage minors from smoking by:

- Pledging to discontinue all free cigarette sampling and distribution of cigarettes through the mail.
- Placing a notice on all packs and cartons of Philip Morris cigarettes stating "Underage Sale Prohibited."
- Distributing minimum age law signage and related materials to over 200,000 retail outlets nationwide.
- Denying merchandising benefits and retail incentives to stores which are fined or convicted of selling cigarettes to minors.

Though touted as a major effort to curtail illegal sale of tobacco to minors, in reality AAA is strictly a publicity campaign, as is now evident from internal industry documents released under court order. AAA came at a time when the Food and Drug Administration (FDA) was proposing to regulate tobacco as a drug and cut down on sales to minors. Moreover, public sentiment had moved strongly against the tobacco industry. It is worth noting that one year after launching the program, not a single merchant had been sanctioned for selling tobacco to minors and there was no evidence that the program had any positive impact whatsoever on youth access to tobacco.

Tobacco Industry Education Programs

- *"The Family C.O.U.R.S.E. Consortium."* Unveiled in 1990, the C.O.U.R.S.E. (Communication Through Understanding, Respect and Self-Esteem) Consortium was created by the Tobacco Institute. The C.O.U.R.S.E. "curriculum" includes two basic components: Distribution of the booklet "Tobacco: Helping Youth Say No" and television Public Service Announcements (PSA's) with the theme "Smoking should not be a part of growing up." Both of these components are produced by the Tobacco Institute.

The themes underlying the C.O.U.R.S.E. "curriculum" or philosophy are familiar:

- Smoking is an adult activity.
- Kids should "refrain" from smoking.
- Adults can choose to smoke, but should discourage their kids from smoking until "they are mature enough."
- There is an enormous amount of peer pressure to smoke.

- *"Helping Youth Say No."* Prepared for the Tobacco Institute by the Family C.O.U.R.S.E. Consortium, this publication is the tobacco industry's major document on youth and tobacco. Subtitled "A Parent's Guide to Helping Teenagers Cope With Peer Pressure," "Helping Youth Say No" provides us with excellent guidance on the tobacco industry's view of what is ineffective in reaching youth.

The major themes which emerge from "Tobacco: Helping Youth Say No," are:

- The major factor in smoking initiation is peer pressure.

- Parents should crack down on teen smoking, even if they themselves smoke.
- Education should be targeted at teens, rather than younger kids.
- Adults can choose to smoke, but should discourage their kids from smoking until "they are mature enough."
- There are many adult activities children shouldn't engage in. Smoking is one of them. They do not yet have the maturity necessary to decide to smoke.

- *"Right Decisions/Right Now."* This program, developed by R.J. Reynolds in 1991, reiterates many of the themes expressed in the Tobacco Institute's "Tobacco: Helping Youth Say No." Program themes include:
  - Smoking is a risk factor, like "many factors statistically associated with an individual's chances of developing disease." This statement makes the tobacco industry seem less ridiculous in denying the health risks of smoking.
  - Kids smoke because of "the power of peer pressure." "Peer pressure is a very strong influence," according to RJR.
  - There are a lot of things adults do that kids shouldn't.

The program has increased in scope over time. RJR is now promoting full-color, glossy materials in schools. The materials offered, free of charge, include posters, brochures for students, and even an "anti-smoking" curriculum. The widely distributed posters are cleverly crafted to contain overt anti-smoking language combined with a visual that contains a subtle pro-smoking message. RJR has also sponsored Right Decisions/Right Now (RD/RN) activities at youth-oriented places. During the 1995 spring break, for example, RJR promoted RD/RN in a booth at a southern California theme park where they distributed RD/RN materials, including RD/RN "pogs," a popular kids' game. RJR also succeeded in getting RD/RN posters placed in a number of feature movies, made-for-TV movies, and popular TV shows, such as Beverly Hills 90210.

Analysis of Ineffective Interventions

An analysis of the tobacco industry's own programs and publications gives us important guidance regarding what the tobacco industry regards as ineffective in anti-tobacco interventions. Because of their sophistication and vast resources, substantial credence should be given to the tobacco industry's assessments, and we recommend steering clear of those strategies and interventions which they embrace.

- *Youth Access.* All of the tobacco industry–backed youth access programs rely on the voluntary cooperation of tobacco retailers. Not surprisingly, these voluntary programs invariably fail to make a dent in youth access. The primary reason for the failure is simple. Tobacco sales to minors are quite lucrative, with youth spending approximately one billion dollars annually on tobacco products. Understandably, merchants are reluctant to forego this source of substantial income. It is also the case that when there is no clear and consistent enforcement of youth access restrictions, merchants often believe that if they were to refuse to sell tobacco to minors, their competitors may still do so.

The problem with the industry backed "youth access" programs is not only that they are ineffective, however. Even if they were to succeed in their stated goal of reducing illegal sales to minors, they would likely still fail to reduce teen tobacco consumption. Teen smoking rates often remain stable even when effective youth access programs are implemented. Unfortunately, the tobacco industry has been highly successful at framing the national tobacco debate as a "kids" issue, and the basic strategy debate as one of reducing youth access.

• *Smoking as an "adult activity."* The tobacco industry portrays smoking as an "adult activity." This is an extremely effective strategy. First, adult activities are by definition attractive to many young people. Second, this strategy lumps smoking in with many other adult activities, such as making one's own choices, which are not inherently harmful. Third, it ignores the addictive nature of nicotine, implying that smoking is simply an adult "choice" or habit, rather than an addiction.

• *Punishing children.* The tobacco industry favors programs and policies penalizing youth for purchasing and possessing cigarettes. The reason for this is obvious—attention is diverted from the tobacco industry's own culpability; blame is shifted onto children and parents. It also lessens the perceived responsibility of merchants. Effective tobacco control policies should avoid all appearance or effect of punishing youth and place responsibility and punishment firmly on the tobacco industry's shoulders.

• *Signage.* The single favorite strategy of the tobacco industry concerning youth is the posting of signs directed at young people. Signs directed at young customers give the message that smoking is an adult initiation. The tobacco industry has identified "'the forbidden fruit' appeal as an important factor in adolescent experimentation" with smoking. Care should be taken in our own policies not to unintentionally redefine the death weed as a forbidden fruit, thereby increasing its attractiveness to youth.

• *Peer pressure.* The tobacco industry fosters a myth of intense, omnipresent peer pressure in the tobacco arena. In reality, most teens and younger kids do not smoke, and environmental cues such as tobacco advertising may be a more important factor in initiation than peer pressure. This is illustrated by the finding that after the massive Joe Camel advertising campaign began, Camel cigarette's market share among underage youth increased from 0.5% in 1988 to 32.8% in 1991.

• *Just Say "No."* The tobacco industry urges youth and parents to "Just Say No" to tobacco (i.e., "Helping Youth Say No"). The industry evidently has determined that this approach to prevention is ineffective. The lesson for our own programs is that we must strive to implement effective prevention programs which unite parents and youth against a common enemy—the tobacco industry.

Ultimately, the primary purpose of the tobacco industry's youth access and tobacco education efforts is simply to divert energy away from interventions that are more effective in preventing tobacco addiction among both children and adults. Such interventions include banning tobacco advertising and promotion, nonsmokers' rights policies (which the Tobacco Institute has identified as "the greatest threat to the viability of the tobacco industry which has yet occurred"), and raising tobacco excise taxes.

Why the War on Tobacco Will Fail

John E. Calfee

In the 1990s, several individuals and groups sued the tobacco industry for health damages claimed to be caused by cigarette smoking. In response to these lawsuits, concerned parties proposed a global settlement which would include tobacco-industry payments to recoup states for the costs of treating smoking-related illnesses and advertising and marketing restrictions that would help reduce teen smoking. John E. Calfee, author of the following selection, argues that these antitobacco efforts will fail to curb teen smoking. In fact, antismoking activists have sabotaged their own efforts by distorting the facts about the causes of smoking and the results of cigarette marketing, he maintains. Ultimately, the author contends, only individuals are responsible for the decision to start—and to quit—smoking. Calfee is a resident scholar at the American Enterprise Institute, a conservative think tank. He is also the author of *Fear of Persuasion: A New Perspective on Advertising and Regulation.*

The war on tobacco has turned upside down. For decades, as new information emerged about the health effects of smoking, public policy relentlessly emphasized individual decision-making. This brought real achievements—notably, a 40 percent reduction in U.S. per capita cigarette consumption between 1975 and 1993.

Some half dozen years ago, however, the battle over tobacco entered a new phase. The focus shifted from smoking to the tobacco industry. A new view took hold. In this view, smoking is caused primarily by deceptive advertising targeted at young people, the manipulation of nicotine to maintain addiction, and the suppression of information on the harm caused by smoking. Smokers should be seen as victims of these forces. And the solution is drastic reform of the industry itself.

This new vision rapidly coalesced into policy. Several states raised tobacco taxes in order to protect smokers from their own preferences

Reprinted, with permission, from "Why the War on Tobacco Will Fail," by John E. Calfee, *The Weekly Standard*, July 20, 1998. Copyright ©1998 by News America Inc.

and to fund anti-smoking campaigns and research. Federal action followed, notably the attempt of the Food and Drug Administration (FDA) to regulate cigarettes as nicotine delivery devices. At the same time came an astonishing barrage of litigation, generating multi-billion-dollar settlements in Mississippi, Texas, Florida, and Minnesota. A June 1997 agreement among plaintiff attorneys, state attorneys general, and the tobacco industry provided a model for comprehensive federal legislative proposals, over which debate continues to this day.

All of this activity tends to focus on a concrete goal and a specific set of tools. The goal is to reduce teen smoking rapidly by half or more, with a corresponding reduction in adult smoking as the teens get older. The tools: elimination of advertising seen by teens, price increases of up to $2 per pack, anti-smoking campaigns, litigation to penalize the industry financially, "look-back" penalties on the industry if teen smoking does not decrease, and FDA jurisdiction over the development of safer cigarettes.

Anti-Smoking Policies Are Failing

The new approach will almost certainly fail. In fact, disturbing symptoms of failure have already begun to appear. Teen smoking has increased substantially since 1991. That has caught people's attention, but probably more alarming is a little-noticed change in the trend of overall consumption. After 15 years of sharp annual declines, per-capita cigarette consumption has hardly dropped since 1993.

Quite aside from these numbers, there are compelling reasons to believe that the central elements of the new plan cannot do what they are supposed to do. Consider prices, the single most important tool in the new thinking. Current proposals would raise federal taxes by a dollar or two—former surgeon general C. Everett Koop and former FDA commissioner David Kessler have proposed $1.50. This is expected to cut teenage smoking by a third or more. The logic is that teens don't realize they will get hooked on nicotine if they smoke, but they will react strongly to higher prices. This seems most unlikely. With teen smokers consuming an average of eight cigarettes a day, there is little reason to expect an extra five or ten cents per cigarette to stop them from smoking. And in fact, the biggest drop in teenage smoking—a nearly one-third decline in the late 1970s—occurred when cigarette prices were also going down (by about 15 percent). On the other hand, prices have been stable or slightly rising since 1991, even as teen smoking increased. In the United Kingdom, where cigarettes already cost twice as much as in the United States, teenagers smoke at about the same rate as they do here.

What about advertising? Tell a teenager that advertising is the reason he smokes, and you will probably convince a teenager that you are out of touch with reality. Repeated statistical analyses have failed to detect a substantial effect on consumption from advertising. One may quibble about the details of individual studies, but the overall results are unmistakable. If advertising's effect on cigarette consumption were substantial, it would have been detected by now.

FDA regulation, if it comes to pass, will be institutionalized frustration. The new rules on advertising cannot reduce teen smoking, because advertising restrictions can hardly prevent what advertising never caused. Safer cigarettes (with less tar and nicotine) will be stymied, as the FDA vigorously implements policies reflecting the public-health community's hostility to safer smoking and new types of cigarettes.

There remain the anti-smoking campaigns. Often tried, they have generally had disappointing results. The people who design these campaigns tend to act on their own pet theories (they think teens are being duped by advertising) and to pursue political goals. Anti-smoking advertising, like the anti-smoking movement generally, has therefore become a vehicle for the new view that the proper target is the tobacco industry rather than smoking.

Thus in California, Massachusetts, and Florida, government-funded campaigns tell kids they can't trust tobacco companies. This non-news is unlikely to cause kids to toss their cigarettes away, but it is consistent with political objectives such as new anti-smoking measures. Two anti-smoking scholars recently praised California's anti-smoking ads for challenging "the dominant view that public health problems reflect personal habits," and they noted that "it is political action and attitudes, rather than personal behavior, on which counter-ads are focused." In fact, the most effective anti-smoking ads probably come from the pharmaceutical firms that market smoking-cessation products. These firms have a financial incentive to communicate the information and strategies that will make people get serious about quitting smoking.

Unsuccessful Strategies

Why do so many well-meaning people pursue measures that cannot achieve their goals? The short answer is that they are prisoners of their own preconceptions. They reject the idea that well-informed people ever choose to smoke; they believe advertising has a power that it has never had; they are ignorant of the history of cigarette marketing; and they give unquestioning credence to economic studies of the "price elasticity" of cigarettes that are of dubious value for the purposes to which they are put.

For the fact is that there is a deep conflict between what anti-smoking campaigners want to be true and what is true. This has fostered a strategy of deception and distortion. Such a strategy can succeed in the short run because of the peculiar circumstances of the tobacco market. Anti-smoking activists learned years ago that when they stretched the facts, those who corrected them were dismissed as industry hacks. This led to the amazing discovery that those who oppose smoking can wander far beyond the boundaries of good science (even in esteemed outlets such as the *Journal of the American Medical Association*) and still see their words accepted and amplified by an unquestioning media. Naturally, anti-smoking campaigners have seized this opportunity, introducing numerous absurdities into the everyday thinking of scholars, regulatory officials, journalists, and politicians. Thus we have been told that cigarettes are the most advertised product in America (wrong by more than an order of magnitude), that research has finally nailed down the connection between marketing and smoking by kids, and that secret industry documents show that the problem all along has been the targeting of youth. Such misinformation is routinely accepted and repeated as if it were the truth.

Here is a concrete example. One of the most often cited *JAMA* studies—in fact, the *only* non-governmental study the FDA cited in its regulatory initiative that actually used market data rather than surveys and the like—claimed to demonstrate that advertising for the first women's brands, in the late 1970s, caused a surge in smoking by teenage girls. The authors used sales data (not advertising data), took their figures from an unpublished student paper, dropped the three of six brands that did not fit their thesis, mistook billions of cigarettes sold for billions of *dollars* worth of cigarettes sold (a forty-fold error), and concluded to much acclaim that massive advertising had fundamentally altered the market. This utterly useless study is repeatedly cited as proof that advertising causes teen smoking. This kind of thing would not happen in an ordinary intellectual environment.

Sometimes, history has been rewritten. Despite what the FDA says, the discovery that people smoke to get nicotine is not new, and neither is the fact that manufacturers strongly influence the amount of nicotine in cigarette smoke. In the late 1960s and early 1970s, maintaining adequate nicotine levels in low-tar cigarettes was widely believed to be the key to progress against the diseases caused by smoking. This belief—which originated with public-health scholars, not the tobacco industry—was so pervasive that Consumer Reports declared in 1972 that "efforts should be made to popularize ways of delivering frequent doses of nicotine to addicts without filling their lungs with smoke."

The National Cancer Institute and the Department of Agriculture maintained a large program devoted to developing improved strains of tobacco (containing more nicotine). A biotech firm hired by a tobacco company to cultivate one of those variants in South America (to avoid growing it in the United States) was recently accused of criminal behavior for doing so in violation of a law that was repealed in 1991. Amazingly, the FDA regarded this episode as a prime justification for regulating the tobacco industry. Again, this kind of thing would not happen in an ordinary intellectual environment.

The Costs of Attacking the Tobacco Industry

Clearly, the new strategy of attacking the tobacco industry rather than smoking is producing little if any benefit. The costs, on the other hand, are large and growing.

First, there are costs to public health. We are abandoning the only approach to smoking-reduction that is likely to succeed: reliance on individual responsibility. This point was eloquently stated by a George Washington University physician, Larry H. Pastor, in a letter to the editor of the *Journal of the American Medical Association* in 1996. Describing the dubious proposition that tobacco litigation will make people quit smoking, Pastor noted that exactly the opposite could easily happen,

> because some smokers will feel reinforced in externalizing blame onto "the tobacco industry" and thereby fail to take the difficult steps necessary to confront their smoking addiction. The more such personal injury litigation succeeds, the more some will comfort themselves with the rationalization that, if they develop tobacco-related illness, they can sue the cigarette makers and obtain a lucrative reward.

The strategy of blaming the industry for smoking is getting in the way of efforts to discourage smoking itself.

Second, there is the matter of who will pay the higher cigarette taxes. A hallmark of the U.S. market is that most smoking is done by people of modest means. And the idea that smokers impose financial costs on others has little foundation. To say that blue-collar smokers should pay more for their habit because they cannot protect themselves from manipulation by the tobacco companies—and then watch them continue to smoke while the nation collects billions of dollars from their pockets to spend on other citizens—is a sorry combination of paternalism and hypocrisy. Perhaps these smokers should simply be allowed to pursue their freely chosen course without financial penalty. At any rate, with teens buying only about 2 percent of the cigarettes sold, we know that a massive tax increase designed to stop teen smoking will be paid almost entirely by non-teens, most of them poor or lower-middle class.

The third cost of the new approach lies in the danger of creating a government stake in continued smoking. The Clinton administration wants to raise cigarette taxes so it can transfer tens of billions of dollars from smokers to its favorite domestic-policy initiatives. Far more dangerous than a mere tax-grab, this plan will work only if most smokers continue to smoke and pay the higher taxes. The public-health community should renounce any such plan. The history of the anti-smoking movement makes clear that the toughest places in which to make progress are countries like Japan, Thailand, and China—that is, nations with a large state investment in smoking. . . .

Finally, the new approach to tobacco carries the cost of degrading the intellectual environment. This is no trivial matter. The public-health community's power depends on information, credibility, and the consequent ability to persuade. That power can be dissipated if it is carelessly misused (as it has been), and once lost, it cannot easily be regained. As journalist Carl Cannon noted, after describing some grossly untrue statements from the White House during the debate over tobacco legislation in the Senate, "The problem is that in employing the devilishly effective—but not always truthful—language of political campaigns, the good guys risk losing the moral high ground." Deception is not—at least should not be, in a free society—a viable long-run strategy.

The time has come, then, for public policy toward tobacco to return to its roots. The only effective way of combating the harmful effects of smoking in the long run is to encourage an enduring sense of personal responsibility—among smokers, their families, and physicians. But that's not all. Two decades of an absurd hostility to safer smoking and safer tobacco must end. We have forgotten that in the 1950s, the pronouncements of cancer researchers created a demand for cigarettes with less tar and nicotine, and the cigarette manufacturers responded with a speed that in hindsight seems miraculous. Today, instead of talking about draconian taxes and sweeping infringements on commercial speech, we should let the competitive market again serve smokers—just as it does everyone else.

REPRESSIVE ANTITOBACCO EFFORTS: THE USE OF TEENS IN STING OPERATIONS

Gian Turci

In the following selection, Gian Turci expresses his anger over the use of teenage informants in "sting" operations intended to catch and punish merchants who sell tobacco to minors. Such tactics, he argues, are frighteningly reminiscent of the kind of state repression that occurs in totalitarian nations. These tactics unduly penalize retailers for errors in judgment, teach youths how to be coercive and disloyal, and foment an atmosphere of distrust in local communities, the author maintains. Moreover, he insists, repressive antismoking efforts actually make cigarettes seem more "dangerous"—and therefore more alluring—to teens. In Turci's opinion, a more effective strategy for reducing youth smoking would be to stop exalting the antitobacco agenda and let smoking rates drop naturally. Turci is an activist in Fighting Ordinances and Restrictions to Control and Eliminate Smoking (FORCES), a smokers' rights organization.

Recently I received from FORCES U.S.A. two articles from San Francisco newspapers, "Minors and Cigarettes" (*San Francisco Chronicle,* Feb. 28/97) and "Teen Smokers Strike Out under New Law" (*San Francisco Examiner,* Feb. 28/97). They detail the deeds of proud teenagers who are helping the police catch merchants who sell tobacco products to minors.

I pride myself for having become callous to the kind of state repression and hysteria going on about tobacco in these times. The San Francisco articles, however, gave me the chills. The training of young people as "bait" for catching merchants during sting operations carries with it a strong odor of "youth education" and "youth heroism" that is Stalinist—not in degree, but certainly in spirit.

Listen to the voice of youth:

"The teen tobacco trend disgusts 16-year-old Isabelle Belkind, one

Reprinted, with permission, from "The Use of Children for Squealing and State Persecution," by Gian Turci, 1997 article on FORCES website: www.forces.org/articles/art-fcan/collabo.htm.

of four students who helped Berkeley police crack down on merchants who sold cigarettes to them," says the article.

"'The point is that we have to inform the merchants that it is not OK to sell (tobacco) to minors,' Belkind said at a press conference outside Berkeley City Hall".

It is interesting that Ms. Belkind chooses (or has been coached to choose) the word "inform" in connection with a sting operation, rather than "enforce," "punish" or "harass." She has been trained well in the art of politically correct verbal hypocrisy.

Teaching Youngsters to Squeal

Here's the program: use youngsters to sting ordinary citizens who are trying to make a living. Teach the kids how to squeal on these people—and possibly ruin them for an error in judgement. Let the youngsters then be rewarded with press coverage and the praise of the state, so that more young people will be encouraged to do the same.

It is appalling to see the kind of effort North American governments put into the elimination of tobacco. Using as justification the usual statistical spin-doctoring, the government employs enormous taxpayer resources in a campaign to satisfy the political needs of the antismoking lobby, supported at the root by irresponsible politicians of the calibre of Bill Clinton, who is seeking the aggrandizement of his popularity through the persecution of an entire class of citizens.

Do the parents of these children have no reservations about the use to which their children are being put? Do they remember the tales of institutionalized youth informants that once emanated from the Soviet Union—usually to widespread distaste in North America? Do they see no parallels? What are we really teaching to the new generation with this? That smoking tobacco is a bad thing? Not particularly. There is a more profound, more general social message that is sent when a method like this is employed.

We are telling young people that reporting on your neighbour is not only acceptable, but laudable and rewarding. As the tobacco wars escalate, we can predict that in the near future this kind of squealing can (and will) be extended as a weapon against parents who smoke in the house. It will be rationalized, of course, on the much publicized "health hazards" of second hand smoke.

Sting Operations Are Counterproductive

The irony of this morally bankrupt approach to "health information" and youth "protection" is that *it won't produce the intended results.* Clearly, the great fanfare about smoking has stimulated the defiance of youth. Teenage smoking is at an all-time high. This is, of course, the result of a grave political error made by the health nazis who are trying to uproot the use of tobacco by the year 2000.

The logical course of action would be to tune down the antismoking fanfare and let long-term smoking rates among the young begin to decline once again—at a natural pace and in the manner set by society in its normal courses. But this requires vision and intelligence, two gifts not very common among antismokers and politicians as they rush against the mysteriously important millenial clock. Instead, in perfect tune with their philosophy, they step up the agenda with the only tool they know: more repression. *Real* education is not even an option at this point.

The "brilliant" idea of stinging business operators has its origin in California, but the Canadian government is rushing to copy the example of the US, now clearly the political "master race".

This is how it works: youngsters who have been properly brain-washed about the dangers of tobacco are now recruited to pose as teenagers eager to get a pack of "smokes". The youngster (who is selected to look much older than his age to facilitate entrapment) gets into the store, asks for cigarettes, and if the poor merchant completes the transaction, it is big trouble, and not only because of the fine. The name and address of the store and its owner can be published in the local newspapers, and a list of stores that have been tagged more than once will soon get posted on the Internet!

The message of the state, and the implied threat, is obvious: We don't fool around with the control of this perfectly legal product. Never mind your common sense: if you make a mistake in assessing the age of an individual, we will punish you, and ruin your business. By publishing your name and address in the media, we will expose you to the danger of community retaliation and vandalism to the extreme consequences.

This isn't far-fetched: the recent "absolution" by a Vancouver, B.C. court of a vandal who threw paint balls on a billboard advertizing a cigarette brand sends the clear message that in these times, damaging property is OK, as long as it is for the good cause of persecuting tobacco.

Making Tobacco a Symbol of Defiance

Of course, none of this nonsense will deter the young from smoking—it will just make the challenge of getting away with it even greater. But it *will* create a whole new breed of "criminals". Young people barely over legal age will go from store to store, armed with I.D., and buy cigarettes for the underaged at a *very lucrative profit*. Unemployed individuals will consider this also, as they discover that this is an easy, non-taxable profit that flows straight into the pocket, and rounds off their incomes. In some B.C. schools, the price for one cigarette is already a dollar. We have elevated tobacco to the status of an exciting drug, and a symbol of defiance.

Common sense indicates that this is not going to work. And the price for this failed attempt will be high, as human nature exploits the opportunity for persecution that has been created. We are teaching our young that ruining an honest businessman is OK: "Why don't we squeal on Joe Blow today, just to see what face he's going to make? He has been rude to me, anyway! And—you know?—perhaps we are even going to make the papers!"

To complete this disgusting scenario, the "sting operation" behaviour will create an environment of distrust among the youth: "Is he a squealer, or even a 'collabo'? Do not smoke when he's around, he may report you."

Or: "Let's not tell anyone where we get the smokes, otherwise they will get stung."

Or even: "I know he's a 'collabo', let's beat the shit out of him!" Not having forgotten the time when I myself was a young teenage boy, I would guess the last option to be the most common, and—to be quite honest—I wouldn't blame the beaters a bit! Kids work out their own rough justice in the school yard.

Damaging Social and Moral Health

In the end, all that we'll obtain from turning our kids into Youth Enforcers is the rationalization of moral, psychological, and physical violence. Politicians and antismokers know that very well, but then the whole idea is meant to intimidate both the youth and adult population for the purpose of dictating the state's will at any cost. Coercion and intimidation are OK when used to impose "what's good for you." *You shall live in fear.*

Using and targeting youth for the purpose of coercion is certainly not a new idea, but until recently, it hasn't been very respectable in North America. Our political class, already devoid of ethics, has acceded to the demands of fanatical groups disguised as health crusaders, and are now filling the new generation's cultural and moral voids with what I call moral antimatter.

While this antimatter may yield some marginal result in the protection of physical health, the cost is the infliction of mortal blows to human, social, and moral health, and the killing of personal choice, freedom, and individualism.

North America wants to present itself to the 21st century clean of all vice—and with this comes a sordid sense of guilt, and contempt for enjoyment at its peak. It's just nasty puritanism with a new face for a new century. In a thoroughly secular and materialistic world, we still yearn for the old redemption, but on terms we can understand: "body" therefore substitutes for "soul", "healthy" substitutes for "holy", and the perfection of the clean and healthy body becomes a rough equivalent to salvation. No matter if the integrity of science is corrupted in the process. No matter if twisted values have been taught to the next generation. It doesn't even matter if North America has to lie to itself, and to the world. The achievement of a long-lived, as well as a controlled and sterile society, is all that matters.

As the great libertarian Pierre Lemieux has foreseen, this new, planned society "will substitute harassment for flirtation, alcoholism for enjoying wine, nicotine delivery devices for cigarettes, and risk for pleasure."

This is the moral inversion, and the spiritual perversion we are passing on to our children.

When a social system rewards the young for hurting their peers; when lies, surveillance and spin-doctoring replace science, honesty and truth in the scale of values, that system doesn't just fall beneath contempt: it slips *beyond repair*. The fate of the Soviet Union has taught nothing to North America. We are now like the ones we once fought.

I thought that many millions of people died—not too long ago—to prevent this shame from ever happening again. I see now I was in error. Here it is, disguised in white coats, stalking the halls of government ministries and health departments, masked as concerned activism and child protection.

As a baby boomer, I am ashamed of my generation, a generation unable to see that the war on tobacco is just the beginning of the war on liberty and choice.

Personally, I'd rather be dead than submit to a society where opinion engineering and state-planned behaviour are the only options. But this is the legacy we leave to our youth.

I just hope that they will have the wisdom to flush it away.

ORGANIZATIONS TO CONTACT

The editors have compiled the following list of organizations concerned with the issues presented in this book. The descriptions are derived from materials provided by the organizations. All have publications or information available for interested readers. The list was compiled on the date of publication of the present volume; the information provided here may change. Be aware that many organizations take several weeks or longer to respond to inquiries, so allow as much time as possible.

Action on Smoking and Health (ASH)
2013 H St. NW, Washington, DC 20006
(202) 659-4310
website: http://www.ash.org

Action on Smoking and Health promotes the rights of nonsmokers and works to protect them from the harms of smoking. ASH has successfully worked to eliminate tobacco ads from radio and television and to ban smoking in airplanes, on buses, and in many public places. The organization publishes the bimonthly newsletter *ASH Smoking and Health Review* and fact sheets on a variety of topics, including teen smoking, passive smoke, and nicotine addiction.

American Cancer Society
1599 Clifton Rd. NE, Atlanta, GA 30329
(800) 227-2345
website: http://www.cancer.org

The American Cancer Society is one of the primary organizations in the United States devoted to educating the public about cancer and to funding cancer research. The society spends a great deal of its resources on educating the public about the dangers of smoking and on lobbying for antismoking legislation. The American Cancer Society makes available hundreds of publications, ranging from reports and surveys to position papers.

American Council on Science and Health (ACSH)
1995 Broadway, 2nd Fl., New York, NY 10023-5860
(212) 362-7044 • fax: (212) 362-4919
e-mail: acsh@acsh.org • website: http://www.acsh.org

ACSH is a consumer education group concerned with issues related to food, nutrition, chemicals, pharmaceuticals, lifestyle, the environment, and health. It publishes the quarterly newsletter *Priorities* as well as the booklets *The Tobacco Industry's Use of Nicotine as a Drug* and *Marketing Cigarettes to Kids*.

Americans for Nonsmokers' Rights
2530 San Pablo Ave., Suite J, Berkeley, CA 94702
(510) 841-3032 • fax: (510) 841-3071
e-mail: anr@no-smoke.org • website: http://www.no-smoke.org

Americans for Nonsmokers' Rights seeks to protect the rights of nonsmokers in the workplace and other public settings. It works with the American Nonsmokers' Rights Foundation, which promotes smoking prevention, nonsmokers' rights, and public education about secondhand smoke. The organization publishes the quarterly newsletter *ANR Update*, the book *Clearing the Air*, and the guidebook *How to Butt In: Teens Take Action*.

American Smokers Alliance (ASA)
PO Box 189, Bellvue, CO 80512
fax: (970) 493-4253
e-mail: derf@smokers.org • website: http://www.smokers.org

The American Smokers Alliance is a nonprofit organization of volunteers who believe that nonsmokers and smokers have equal rights. ASA strives to unify existing smokers' rights efforts, combat anti-tobacco legislation, fight discrimination against smokers in the workplace, and encourage individuals to become involved in local smokers' rights movements. It publishes articles and news bulletins, including "Smokers Have Reduced Risks of Alzheimer's and Parkinson's Disease" and "Lung Cancer Can Be Eliminated!"

Canadian Council for Tobacco Control (CCTC)
170 Laurier Ave. W, Suite 1000, Ottawa, ON K1P 5V5 CANADA
(800) 267-5234 • (613) 567-3050 • fax: (613) 567-5695
e-mail: info-services@cctc.ca • website: http://www.cctc.ca/ncth

The CCTC works to ensure a healthier society, free from addiction and involuntary exposure to tobacco products. It promotes a comprehensive tobacco control program involving educational, social, fiscal, and legislative interventions. It publishes several fact sheets, including "Promoting a Lethal Product" and "The Ban on Smoking on School Property: Successes and Challenges."

Children Opposed to Smoking Tobacco (COST)
Mary Volz School, 509 W. 3rd Ave., Runnemede, NJ 08078
(609) 931-5353 • fax: (609) 931-1827
e-mail: costkids@costkids.org • website: http://www.costkids.org

COST was founded in 1996 by a group of middle school students committed to keeping tobacco products out of the hands of children. Much of the organization's efforts are spent fighting the tobacco industry's advertising campaigns directed at children and teenagers. Articles such as "Environmental Tobacco Smoke," "What Is a Parent to Do?," and "What You Can Do" are available on its website.

Competitive Enterprise Institute (CEI)
1001 Connecticut Ave. NW, Suite 1250, Washington, DC 20036
(202) 331-1010 • fax: (202) 331-0640
e-mail: info@cei.org • website: http://www.cei.org

The institute is a pro–free market public interest group that addresses a wide range of issues, including tobacco. CEI questions the validity and accuracy of Environmental Protection Agency studies that report the dangers of secondhand smoke. Its publications include books, monographs, policy studies, and the monthly newsletter *CEI Update*.

Environmental Protection Agency (EPA)
Indoor Air Quality Information Clearinghouse
PO Box 37133, Washington, DC 20013-7133
(800) 438-4318 • (202) 484-1307 • fax: (202) 484-1510
e-mail: iaqinfo@aol.com • website: http://www.epa.gov/iaq

The EPA is the agency of the U.S. government that coordinates actions designed to protect the environment. It promotes indoor air quality standards that reduce the dangers of secondhand smoke. The EPA publishes and distributes reports such as "Respiratory Health Effects of Passive Smoking: Lung Cancer and Other Disorders" and "What You Can Do About Secondhand Smoke as Parents, Decisionmakers, and Building Occupants."

Fight Ordinances & Restrictions to Control & Eliminate Smoking (FORCES)
PO Box 591257, San Francisco, CA 94159
(415) 824-4716
e-mail: info@forces.org • website: http://www.forces.org

FORCES fights against smoking ordinances and restrictions designed to eventually eliminate smoking, and it works to increase public awareness of smoking-related legislation. It opposes any state or local ordinance it feels is not fair to those who choose to smoke. Although FORCES does not advocate smoking, it asserts that an individual has the right to choose to smoke and that smokers should be accommodated where and when possible. FORCES publishes *Tobacco Weekly* as well as many articles.

Group Against Smoking Pollution (GASP)
PO Box 632, College Park, MD 20741-0632
(301) 459-4791

Consisting of nonsmokers adversely affected by tobacco smoke, GASP works to promote the rights of nonsmokers, to educate the public about the problems of secondhand smoke, and to encourage the regulation of smoking in public places. The organization provides information and referral services and distributes educational materials, buttons, posters, and bumper stickers. GASP publishes booklets and pamphlets such as *The Nonsmokers' Bill of Rights* and *The Nonsmokers' Liberation Guide*.

National Center for Tobacco-Free Kids/Campaign for Tobacco-Free Kids
1707 L St. NW, Suite 800, Washington, DC 20036
(800) 284-5437
e-mail: info@tobaccofreekids.org • website: http://www.tobaccofreekids.org

The National Center for Tobacco-Free Kids/Campaign for Tobacco-Free Kids is the largest private initiative ever launched to protect children from tobacco addiction. The center works in partnership with the American Cancer Society, American Heart Association, American Medical Association, the National PTA and more than one hundred other health, civic, corporate, youth, and religious organizations. Among the center's publications are press releases, reports, and fact sheets, including "Tobacco Use Among Youth," "Tobacco Marketing to Kids," and "Smokeless (Spit) Tobacco and Kids."

U.S. Food and Drug Administration (FDA)
Rockville, MD 20857
(800) 532-4440 • (301) 443-1130 • fax: (301) 443-9767
e-mail: execsec@oc.fda.gov • website: http://www.fda.gov

As the agency of the U.S. government charged with protecting the health of the public against impure and unsafe foods, drugs, cosmetics, and other potential hazards, the FDA has sought the regulation of nicotine as a drug and has investigated manipulation of nicotine levels in cigarettes by the tobacco industry. It provides copies of congressional testimony given in the debate over the regulation of nicotine.

BIBLIOGRAPHY

Books

William Everett Bailey	*The Invisible Drug.* Cincinnati, OH: Mosaic, 1996.
John C. Burnham	*Bad Habits: Drinking, Smoking, Taking Drugs, Sexual Misbehavior, and Swearing in America.* New York: New York University Press, 1993.
Karen Casey	*If Only I Could Quit: Recovering from Nicotine Addiction.* Center City, MN: Hazelden, 1995.
John Fahs	*Cigarette Confidential: The Unfiltered Truth About the Ultimate American Addiction.* New York: Berkeley, 1996.
Gladys Folkers and Jeanne Engelmann	*Taking Charge of My Mind and Body: A Girls' Guide to Outsmarting Alcohol, Drugs, Smoking, and Eating Problems.* Minneapolis: Free Spirit, 1997.
Stanton A. Glantz	*The Cigarette Papers.* Berkeley and Los Angeles: University of California Press, 1996.
Peter D. Jacobson	*Tobacco Control Laws: Implementation and Enforcement.* Santa Monica, CA: RAND, 1997.
Richard Klein	*Cigarettes Are Sublime.* Durham, NC: Duke University Press, 1994.
Richard Kluger	*Ashes to Ashes: America's Hundred-Year Cigarette War, the Public Health, and the Unabashed Triumph of Philip Morris.* New York: Knopf, 1996.
Susan S. Lang and Beth H. Marks	*Teens and Tobacco: A Fatal Attraction.* New York: Twenty-First Century Books, 1996.
Barbara S. Lynch and Richard J. Bonnie, eds.	*Growing Up Tobacco Free: Preventing Nicotine Addiction in Children and Youths.* Washington, DC: National Academy Press, 1994.
Daniel McMillan	*Teen Smoking: Understanding the Risk.* Springfield, NJ: Enslow, 1997.
Jacob Sullum	*For Your Own Good: The Anti-Smoking Crusade and the Tyranny of Public Health.* New York: Free Press, 1998.
W. Kip Viscusi	*Smoking: Making the Risky Decision.* New York: Oxford University Press, 1993.
Elizabeth M. Whelan, ed.	*Cigarettes: What the Warning Label Doesn't Tell You: The First Comprehensive Guide to the Health Consequences of Smoking.* Amherst, NY: Prometheus Books, 1997.

Periodicals

Jonathan Alter	"Smoking Out What's Cool," *Newsweek,* June 30, 1997.
George J. Annas	"Cowboys, Camels, and the First Amendment—the FDA's Restrictions on Tobacco Advertising," *New England Journal of Medicine,* December 5, 1996. Available from 10 Shattuck St., Boston, MA 02115-6094.

Ernest Beck	"Ad Bans Abroad Haven't Snuffed Out Smoking," *Wall Street Journal*, June 12, 1997.
Kirsten Conover	"Keeping Kids from Lighting Up," *Christian Science Monitor*, July 29, 1998.
Consumer Reports	"Hooked on Tobacco: The Teen Epidemic," March 1995.
Consumer Reports	"Seductive Cigars: New Ways to Addict the Next Generation," May 1998.
Tammerlin Drummond	"Busted for Possession," *Time*, December 7, 1998.
Christopher John Farley	"C'mon Baby, Light My Fire," *Time*, January 27, 1997.
Terry Golway	"Life in the '90s," *America*, December 12, 1998.
Ginny Graves	"Teen Smoking: Helping Kids Quit," *American Health for Women*, January/February 1997.
Issues and Controversies on File	"Tobacco Settlement," November 20, 1998. Available from Facts On File News Services, 11 Penn Plaza, New York, NY 10001-2006.
Kathiann Kowalski	"Tobacco's Toll on Teens," *Current Health*, February 1997.
John Leo	"Boyz to (Marlboro) Men," *U.S. News & World Report*, June 2, 1997.
John J. Lynch and Thomas Humber	"Do We Need a Tobacco Bill?" *World & I*, July 1998. Available from 3600 New York Ave. NE, Washington, DC 20002.
Barbara Martinez	"Antismoking Ads Aim to Gross Out Teens," *Wall Street Journal*, March 31, 1997.
John McCain	"A Defeat for the Nation's Children," *America*, August 15–22, 1998.
John McCain and Robert A. Levy	"Q: Should Congress Decide the Future of the Tobacco Industry?" *Insight*, May 11, 1998. Available from 3600 New York Ave. NE, Washington, DC 20002.
Barry Meier	"Politics of Youth Smoking Fueled by Unproven Data," *New York Times*, May 20, 1998.
Michele Mitchell	"Why Young People Still Smoke," *New York Times*, August 4, 1997.
Mireya Navarro	"Florida Gives Teen-Age Smokers a Day in Court," *New York Times*, July 20, 1998.
Mark Naymik	"After Joe Camel," *Washington Post National Weekly Edition*, September 22, 1997. Available from Reprints, 1150 15th St. NW, Washington, DC 20071.
William D. Novelli	"Tobacco Control: The Dramatic Choice," *Science*, October 10, 1997.
Marc Peyser	"Cool Fools," *Newsweek*, July 21, 1997.

Andres C. Revkin   "Herbal Tobacco Substitutes on Rise and So Are
                            Worries," *New York Times*, May 24, 1998.

Joseph P. Shapiro   "Industry Foes Fume over Tobacco Deal," *U.S. News &
                            World Report*, November 30, 1998.

Patricia Sosa   "Kids Kicking Butts," *Christian Social Action*, June
                            1998. Available from 100 Maryland Ave. NE,
                            Washington, DC 20002.

Geoffrey Stevens   "Stopping Kids from Smoking," *Maclean's*, August 24,
                            1998.

Jacob Sullum   "Cowboys, Camels, and Kids: Does Advertising Turn
                            People into Smokers?" *Reason*, April 1998.

David Tannenbaum   Special issue on the Tobacco Papers, *Multinational
and Robert Weissman   Monitor*, July/August 1998.

Mike Thomas   "Just Trying to Be Cool," *Reader's Digest*, March 1997.

Julie VanTine   "Stogie-Smoking Teens?" *Prevention*, December 1997.

Elizabeth M. Whelan   "Is a Deal with the Cigarette Industry in the Interest
                            of Public Health?" *Priorities*, vol. 9, no. 2, 1997.
                            Available from the American Council on Science and
                            Health, 1995 Broadway, 2nd Fl., New York, NY 10023-
                            5860.

INDEX